P9-CBI-909

BAPTIST

CHURCH MANUAL

By J. M. PENDLETON, D. D.

Let all things be done decently and in order.—1 Cor. 14 : 40

BROADMAN PRESS

NASHVILLE, TENNESSEE

CONTENTS

INDEX

CHURCH MANUAL

CHAPTER I

NATURE OF A CHURCH

THE term *Church* occurs in the New Testament more than a hundred times. The word thus translated means congregation or assembly; but it does not indicate the purpose for which the congregation or assembly meets. Hence it is used, Acts 19 : 32, 39, 41, and rendered *assembly*. In every other place in the New Testament it is translated *church*. In its application to the followers of Christ, it refers either to a particular congregation of saints, or to the redeemed in the aggregate. It is employed in the latter sense in Ephesians 1 : 22; 3 : 21; 5 : 25, 27. Here we have the expressions, " Head over all things to the Church"; " To him be glory in the Church by Christ Jesus throughout all ages world without end"; " Christ loved the Church and

5

gave himself for it . . . that he might present it to himself a glorious Church, not having spot or wrinkle or any such thing; but that it should be holy and without blemish." In these passages, and a few more like them, it would be absurd to define the term Church as meaning a particular congregation of Christians, meeting in one place for the worship of God.

Our business, however, is with the other signification of the word church. In a large majority of instances it is used in the Scriptures to denote a local assembly, convened for religious purposes. Thus we read of "the church at Jerusalem," "the church of God which is at Corinth," "the church of the Thessalonians," "the church of Ephesus," "the church in Smyrna," "the church in Pergamus," etc., etc. Nor are we to suppose that it required a large number of persons to constitute a church. Paul refers to Aquila and Priscilla and "the church that is in their house," to Nymphas and "the church which is in his house," and in his letter to Philemon he says, "to the church in thy house." A congregation of saints, organized according to the New Testament, whether that congregation is large or small, is a church.

The inspired writers, as if to preclude the idea of a church commensurate with a province, a kingdom, or an empire, make use of the following forms of expression, " the *churches* of Galatia," " the *churches* of Macedonia," " the *churches* of Asia," " the *churches* of Judea "; but they never say the *church* of Galatia, the *church* of Macedonia, etc. Wherever Christianity prevailed in apostolic times there was a plurality of churches.

In answer to the question, What is a church? it may be said: A church is a congregation of Christ's baptized disciples, acknowledging him as their Head, relying on his atoning sacrifice for justification before God, and depending on the Holy Spirit for sanctification, united in the belief of the gospel, agreeing to maintain its ordinances and obey its precepts, meeting together for worship, and cooperating for the extension of Christ's kingdom in the world. If any prefer an abridgment of the definition it may be given thus: A church is a congregation of Christ's baptized disciples, united in the belief of what he has said, and covenanting to do what he has commanded.

If this be a correct description of a church of Christ, it is manifest that membership must be preceded by important qualifications. These qualifications may be considered as *moral* and *ceremonial*.

MORAL. Among moral prerequisites to church-membership may be mentioned

Repentance. John the Baptist, whose ministry was " the beginning of the gospel of Jesus Christ," preached, saying to the people, " Repent ye ; for the kingdom of heaven is at hand." His was the baptism of repentance. When John was cast into prison Jesus " came into Galilee, preaching the gospel of the kingdom of God, and saying, " The time is fulfilled, and the kingdom of God is at hand : repent ye and believe the gospel." When the apostles were sent forth they " preached that men should repent." The Lord Jesus after his resurrection said : " Thus it is written and thus it behooved Christ to suffer and to rise from the dead the third day, and that repentance and remission of sins should be preached in his name among all nations." Peter on the day of Pentecost said, " Repent and be baptized every one of you in the name of Jesus Christ for the remission of sins " ; and Paul, who testified at Ephesus for three years " repentance toward God and faith toward our Lord Jesus Christ," proclaimed in Athens, "God commandeth all men everywhere to repent." The New Testament is full of the doctrine of repentance. It is a doctrine of the gospel. The law knows nothing of it. The language of the law is, Do and live—not Repent, that you may be pardoned. Repentance involves such a change of mind in regard to sin as is indispensable to a proper appreciation of the blessings of the kingdom of Christ. Hence no impenitent sinner can constitutionally enter into the kingdom. There is no place more inappropriate for the impenitent than a church of Christ.

Faith. This is another moral qualification for church-membership. Great importance is in the Scriptures attached to faith in Christ, as will appear from the following passages: "He that believeth on him is not condemned." "He that believeth on the Son hath everlasting life." "These things are written that ye may believe that Jesus is the Christ, the Son of God, and that believing ye may have life through his name." "He that believeth and is baptized shall be saved." "By him all that believe are justified from all things." "Whom God hath set forth as a propitiation through faith in his blood . . . that he might be just and the justifier of him that believeth in Jesus." " Therefore being justified by faith, we have peace with God through our Lord Jesus Christ."

These passages, with many others, clearly show that in the economy of the gospel faith in Christ is recognized as an essential principle. Why is this? Not because faith is a meritorious exercise. There is, there can be, no merit in it. This is evident, because faith is a duty, and there can be no merit in the performance of a duty. But, while faith possesses no merit, it brings the soul into vital contact with the blood of atonement, which possesses infinite merit. It unites to Christ. Its province is to receive Christ, and with him all the blessings of the " new covenant." Christ is emphatically the object of faith. The faith which avails to salvation has respect to him and embraces him.

Faith in Christ—the faith which instrumentally achieves the sinner's justification before God—is an essential qualification for church-membership. No unbeliever has the shadow of a claim to citizenship in the kingdom of Christ. The formal mention of regeneration as a prerequisite to church-membership has been omitted, because it necessarily co-exists with repentance and faith. Every penitent believer is a regenerate person. Regeneration is the spiritual process by which we become new creatures in Christ—are born again—born of the Spirit—born of God—quickened together with Christ—renewed after the image of God, etc., etc. "Ye are all the children of God by faith in Christ Jesus," is the language of Paul to the Galatians; and the beloved disciple says, "Whosoever believeth that Jesus is the Christ, is born of God." If faith therefore, as we have seen, is a qualification for church-membership, regeneration must be also; for it is so inseparable from faith, that every one who believes in Christ is born of God. And it follows, that if faith is a prerequisite to baptism, regeneration is likewise. This being the case, regeneration does not occur in baptism.

Let it never be forgotten that the only suitable materials of which to construct a church of Christ, so far as spiritual qualifications are concerned, are regenerate, penitent, believing persons. To make use of other materials is to subvert the fundamental principles of church organization. It is to destroy the kingdom of Christ; for how can there be a kingdom without subjects—such subjects as the King requires?

It is a regulation of the Head of the Church that his spiritual subjects be organized into visible, local communities. We read therefore. in the New Testament, of churches—another name for these communities. There are frequent references to local congregations. These congregations had a regular, visible organization; and there must have been some visible act of initiation into them. What was it? This leads to a consideration of

2. *The ceremonial qualification for church-membership.* This qualification is baptism. There can, according to the Scriptures, be no visible church without baptism. An observance of this ordinance is the believer's first public act of obedience to Christ. Regeneration, repentance, and faith are private matters between God and the soul. They involve internal piety, but of this piety there must be an external manifestation. This manifestation is made in baptism. The penitent, regenerate believer is baptized into the name of the Father, and of the Son, and of the Holy Spirit. There is a visible, symbolic expression of a

new relationship to the three persons of the Godhead—a relationship entered into in repentance, faith, and regeneration. We are said to be baptized into the death of Christ. We profess our reliance on his death for salvation; and we emblematically declare that as he died *for* sin, so we have died *to* sin, and have risen from our death in trespasses and sins to newness of life. We solemnly commemorate the burial and resurrection of the Lord Jesus, and are ourselves symbolically buried to the world. In baptism our sins are *declaratively* remitted—*formally* washed away. Washing in water frees the body from literal impurity. Baptism is a *symbolic* release of the soul from the defilement of sin. There is an *actual,* a *real* remission of sins when we believe in Christ—there is a *declarative, formal, symbolic* remission in baptism.

That the views, now presented, of the moral and ceremonial qualifications for church membership are in accordance with the New Testament will be seen by referring to the commission of Christ, as understood and executed by the apostles, on the day of Pentecost. The commission said, " Go, teach [make disciples of] all nations, baptizing them in the name of the Father, and of the Son, and of the Holy Spirit: teaching them to observe all things, whatsoever I have commanded you." A great awakening took place under Peter's preaching, and repenting thousands accepted salvation through Christ. It is added, " Then they that gladly received his word were baptized: and the same day there were added unto them about three thousand souls." Subsequently it is said, " The Lord added to the church daily such as should be saved." The converts to the faith were first baptized and then added to the church. This shows baptism to be prerequisite to church-membership. It was so regarded at Jerusalem on the day of Pentecost, when the apostles began to act under the commission of their risen Lord; and it is morally certain it was so regarded wherever they established churches. And as churches in all ages must be formed after the apostolic model, it follows that where penitent, regenerate, baptized believers in Christ are found, there are scriptural materials for a church. Such persons having first given themselves to the Lord, and then to one another, in solemn covenant, agreeing to make the will of Christ as expressed in his word their rule of action, are, in the New Testament sense of the term, a *church*. Whether they are many or few in number, they are a church. But in the absence of penitent, regenerate, baptized believers in Christ, there cannot be a New Testament church.

CONSTITUTION OF CHURCHES

When the interests of Christ's kingdom require the formation of a new church the customary mode of procedure is about this: Brethren and sisters obtain letters of dismission from the church or churches to which they belong, for the purpose of entering into the new organization. It is well for this purpose to be stated in the letters. When they meet together at the appointed time, a Moderator and Clerk *pro tem* are appointed. The meeting is opened with devotional exercises. Sometimes a sermon is preached. especially when it is not intended to have recognition services at some future day. Reading the Scriptures and prayer should be considered indispensable. This being done, the letters of dismission are read, and the parties concerned resolve by solemn vote to consider themselves an independent church. What is called a church covenant is adopted, as also Articles of Faith. These Articles of Faith are not intended as, in any sense, a substitute for the word of God; but only as an expression of the views of the constituent members as to the prominent teachings of the Scriptures. It is very important to the peace, efficiency, and usefulness of a church that there be among its members substantial harmony of sentiment as to what the Bible teaches. Differences of opinion on little matters, so regarded, have sometimes illustrated the truth of the inspired exclamation, " Behold, how great a matter a little fire kindleth ! " It would have saved hundreds of churches a great deal of trouble, if they had remembered, at the right time, that neither two nor any other number, can walk together, except they be agreed. Ordinarily, a church at the time of its constitution, selects a name by which it is to be designated, and appoints its officers. This, however, is not indispensable. It is sometimes best, for prudential reasons, to defer the election of officers.

RECOGNITION OF CHURCHES

The same importance is not to be attached to the recognition as to the constitution of a church. It is not necessary to the validity of church organization Still, the advantages resulting from a suitable recognition should not be lightly esteemed. It adds much to the influence of a new church to be cordially endorsed and welcomed into the sisterhood of churches. This is usually done by a council of recognition, composed of ministers and others from churches in the vicinity. Sometimes councils examine very closely the facts connected with the formation of new churches, Articles of Faith, etc.; but generally are so well satisfied as to make no special investigation. Recognition services usually embrace Reading the Scriptures, Prayer, Sermon, giving the Hand of Fellowship, and a Charge to the Church.

HOW MEMBERS ARE RECEIVED

There are two ways of receiving members into a church.

1. *By Experience and Baptism.* 2. *By Letters of Dismission* from sister churches. In accordance with the first way, persons wishing to unite with a church give an account of the dealings of God with their souls, and state the " reason of the hope that is in them "; where-

upon, if, in the judgment of the church they " have passed from death unto life," they are by vote of the church recognized as candidates for baptism, with the understanding that when baptized they will be entitled to all the rights and privileges of membership. Great care should be exercised in receiving members. Many churches err at this point. They do not observe the requisite caution; for they receive persons who give, to say the least, very imperfect evidence of piety. There is much danger of this, especially in times of religious excitement. Pastors should positively assure themselves that those who are received for baptism have felt themselves to be guilty, ruined, helpless sinners, justly condemned by God's holy law; and under a sense of their lost condition have trusted in Christ for salvation. After baptism—usually at the first celebration of the Lord's Supper—it is the general, and should be the universal custom for the pastor to give the hand of fellowship to the newly baptized, in token of their having been received into full membership. This affords the pastor a suitable opportunity of saying something as to the import and obligations of the Christian profession.

The other way of becoming members of a church is by presenting Letters of Dismission from sister churches. These letters affording satisfactory proof of their Christian character and standing, the applicants for membership are received and the hand of fellowship given, as in the former case. It is proper to say that by *sister* churches are meant churches of similar faith and order. Hence no Baptist church can receive and recognize, as a passport to membership, a letter from any Pedobaptist organization. There is such a lack of similar faith and order as to render this utterly inadmissible. It sometimes happens that persons who have been baptized where there is no church, and persons who, owing to the extinction of the church to which they belonged, or to other circumstances, find themselves without regular Letters of Dismission, wish to enjoy the privileges of membership. In such cases it is only necessary for the church applied to to be satisfied of the worthiness of the applicants, and they are received.

HOW MEMBERSHIP CEASES

Membership in a church terminates in three ways.

1. *By Death*. The dead can have no place in any earthly congregation of the saints.

2. *By Exclusion*. A church has the right, according to the Scriptures, and is under obligation to exclude from its fellowship any member who holds heretical doctrines, or lives inconsistently with the Christian profession. More will be said on this subject in the Chapter on Discipline.

3. *By Dismission*. Letters of Dismission are granted to members who apply for them, provided they are in good standing. The fact that disciplinary proceedings have not been instituted against a member is generally to be taken as an evidence of good standing; and, therefore, of a right to a letter of dismission. There are, however, some exceptional cases. A member who asks for a letter of dismission with the purpose of evading church discipline, because he has reason to expect it, has no right to a letter. Such a case must be investigated. The general rule would be to grant a letter to the member who asks for it, provided he would not be subject to discipline if he did not ask for it. The time at which a dismissed member ceases to be a member depends on the church that grants the letter. Some churches con-

sider the connection as terminated as soon as a letter is granted. The great majority of churches, however, and very properly, regard dismissed members as under their jurisdiction until they are received into other churches. Some churches have a way a getting clear of members by a process which is called " *dropping*." This is considered less disgraceful than exclusion, and is resorted to chiefly in the case of members who for a long time, willingly, absent themselves from the meetings of the church, or have gone, the church knows not where. The *dropping* process is unnecessary. It differs but little from exclusion—not at all in its effects. That is to say, the *dropped* as well as the *excluded* are no longer church-members. It may be said too, that members who habitually stay away from the house of God deserve *exclusion,* as do those who, not prizing church privileges as they ought, emigrate to other places without asking for Letters of Dismission.

CHAPTER II

IT cannot be said that officers are essential to the *existence* of a church; for a church must exist before it can appoint its officers. After this appointment, if, in the providence of God, they should be removed by death, it might affect the interests, but not the *being* of the church. It has been well said by an able writer, that " although officers are not necessary to the *being* of a church, they are necessary to its *well-being*." No church can reasonably expect to prosper which does not obey the law of its Head in regard to the appointment of officers. It is obvious too, from the teachings of the New Testament, that pastors and deacons are the scriptural officers of Christian churches Paul, referring to Christ's ascension gifts, says : " And he gave some, apostles; and some, prophets; and some, evangelists; and some, pastors and teachers; for the perfecting of the saints, for the work of the ministry, for the

edifying of the body of Christ" (Eph. 4 :
11, 12). Apostles, prophets, and evangelists
filled extraordinary and temporary offices.
There are no such offices now. Pastors and
deacons are the spiritual officers of the
churches. The New Testament leaves room
for churches to have other officers as needed,
but pastors and deacons are the two kinds of
officers that each church should have.

I. PASTOR. This term was first applied to
ministers having oversight of churches, because there is a striking analogy between such
a minister and a literal shepherd. A shepherd
has under his charge a flock, for which he
must care, and for whose wants he must provide. The sheep and the lambs must be looked
after. The Lord Jesus, " the great Shepherd
of the sheep," the chief Shepherd, virtually
says to all his under-shepherds, as he did to
Peter, " Feed my sheep," " Feed my lambs."
It is worthy of remark that this language was
not addressed to Peter till the Saviour obtained
from him an affirmative answer to the question
three times propounded, " Lovest thou me? "
As if he had said, " I love my spiritual flock
so well, I cannot entrust the sheep and lambs

composing it to any man who does not love me." And love to Christ must be regarded in all ages and in all places as the pastor's supreme qualification. All other qualifications are worthless if this is absent. Talent and learning are not to be undervalued; but they must be kept under the control of piety, and receive its sanctifying impress. With regard to the pastoral office, there are two things worthy of special consideration.

1. *The Work of Pastors.* Truly theirs is a work. Paul says, "If any man desire the office of a bishop, he desireth a good work." It is indeed a good work—the best work on earth—but a *work*. We must not suffer the term bishop to suggest any such idea as the word in its modern acceptation implies. In apostolic times there were no bishops having charge of the churches of a district of country, a province, or a kingdom. A bishop was a pastor of a church, and the New Testament, so far from encouraging a plurality of churches under one pastor, refers, in two instances at least, to a plurality of pastors in one church. (See Acts 20 : 28; Phil. 1 : 1.) In the former passage the elders of the church at Ephesus are called *overseers,* and the word

thus translated is the same rendered *bishop* in Philippians 1 : 1 ; 1 Timothy 3 : 2 ; Titus 1 : 7 ; 1 Peter 2 : 25. Thus does it appear that pastor, bishop, and elder are three terms designating the same office. This view is further confirmed by a reference to Peter 5 : 1, 2, where elders are exhorted to feed the flock— that is, to perform the office of pastor or shepherd—taking the oversight thereof, etc.—that is, acting the part of bishops or overseers. For the word translated *taking the oversight* belongs to the same family of words as the term rendered bishop in the passages cited. It is plain, therefore, that a pastor's work is the spiritual oversight of the flock, the church he serves. Like a good literal shepherd he must care for the feeble and the sick, as well as for the healthy and the vigorous. Some he can feed with " strong food," while others can digest nothing stronger than " milk." He must exercise a sanctified discretion, and " *study* to show himself approved to God, a workman that needeth not to be ashamed, rightly dividing the word of truth." Much depends on dividing the word of truth *rightly;* and hence the necessity of study— prayerful study, imbued with the spirit of the Master. The administration of ordinances as well as the preaching of the word is the proper business of the pastor. It does not accord with the plan of this volume to elaborate any topic, and therefore the work of the pastor cannot be enlarged on, nor is there room to present the many motives to pastoral fidelity. The mention of two must suffice: the church, over whose interest the pastor watches, has been "bought with the precious blood of Christ"; and the faithful pastor will, when "the chief Shepherd" comes, "receive a crown of glory that fadeth not away." What motives to diligence and faithfulness could possess more exhaustless power!

2. *The Authority of Pastors.* All things earthly are liable to abuse, and that feature of congregational church government which places all the members on an equality in the transaction of church business, has been, in some instances at least, suffered to interfere with the deference due to pastors. There is a class of Scriptures whose import is not sufficiently considered—such as the following: "And we beseech you, brethren, to know them which labor among you, and are over you in the Lord, and admonish you; and to esteem

them very highly in love for their work's sake." "Let the elders that rule well be counted worthy of double honor, especially they who labor in the word and doctrine." "Remember them which have the rule over you, who have spoken to you the word of God." "Obey them that have the rule over you, and submit yourselves: for they watch for your souls, as they that must give account." In these passages pastors are referred to, and there is claimed for them an authority not belonging to other church-members. They are to be esteemed highly for their work's sake. Whatever esteem their personal merits may excite, they are to be chiefly esteemed for the great and glorious work in which they are enagaged. On account of this work they are to be regarded worthy of "double honor," that is, special honor. This surely is reasonable, for pastors are chosen by the churches over which they preside. The churches act voluntarily, and the love which prompts the choice of a pastor should secure for him reverential respect in the performance of his duties. The words *rule, obey,* and *submit* in the foregoing quotations mean something. The ruling is not unrestricted, neither is the obedience and submission. The pastor is to rule *in accordance with the law of Christ.* No other kind of rule is legitimate or obligatory; but when he rules in accordance with the will of Christ, obedience and submission on the part of the members of the church are imperative duties. Andrew Fuller well says, " It is in this view, as teaching *divine* truth, and enforcing *divine* commands, that the servants of God, in all ages, have been invested with divine authority." [1] It may be added that this is the only sense in which men can be invested with divine authority.

Distinguished scholars are of opinion that the two passages quoted, which refer to ruling, should be translated thus: "Remember your leaders," etc. " Obey your leaders," etc. Admitting the correctness of this rendering—and it cannot be denied—still the idea would not be essentially different. Pastors in leading their flocks do, in one sense, rule them; and in the only sense in which they should rule them. While the proper exercise of pastoral authority is essential to the spiritual welfare of a church, pastors must beware of assuming a power which does not belong to them. They

[1] Complete Works, Vol. I, p. 197.

must remember the words of Peter: "Neither as being lords over God's heritage, but being examples to the flock." There must be, in the exercise of pastoral authority, nothing like priestly lordship or clerical despotism; but the influence of pastors must grow out of the fact that *they* faithfully obey the will of Christ, the great Shepherd, and thus set an example worthy of imitation. There is nothing which gives a pastor so much influence as unreserved consecration to the work of the Lord. As the influence of judicious pastors increases the more they are known, the pastoral relation should be rendered as permanent as possible. It should not be dissolved for any slight cause. As to the custom of some churches that choose their pastors annually, it would be difficult to say too much in condemnation of it. It is vastly injurious both to pastors and churches. Pastors should be chosen for an indefinite period. If the work of the Lord prospers under their labors, well; if they find after a sufficient trial, that they are not accomplishing good, let them resign.

II. DEACONS. A prototype of the office of deacon appeared in early church life in the sixth chapter of the Acts of the Apostles. It is said that " when the number of the disciples was multiplied, there arose a murmuring of the Grecians against the Hebrews, because their widows were neglected in the daily ministration." The " Grecians " were Jews as well as the Hebrews, but they spoke the Greek language, and were probably not natives of Palestine. The members of the church at Jerusalem " had all things in common," and a distribution was made out of the common stock " as every man had need." This seems to have been done at first under the immediate direction of the apostles; and the intimation is that the large increase of the church interfered with an impartial distribution of supplies. The apostles saw that, if they made it their personal business to " serve tables," it would greatly hinder their work in its spiritual aspects. They said: " It is not reason that we should leave the word of God, and serve tables; wherefore, brethren, look ye out among you seven men of honest report, full of the Holy Spirit and wisdom, whom we may appoint over this business. But we will give ourselves continually to prayer, and to the ministry of the word."

Thus the creation of the office of deacon recognizes the fact that the duties of pastors are preeminently spiritual; and that they should not be overburdened with other interests of the churches. The opinion has been entertained by some that the deaconship was designed to be temporary. The argument is that the office was created because the property of the church at Jerusalem had been thrown together into a common stock, and it was requisite to have officers to superintend and distribute it. Then the inference is drawn, that when the property of church-members was no longer put into a common stock, the office of deacon was virtually abolished. This reasoning is more plausible than conclusive. In proof of this it may be said, that the members of the church at Jerusalem were not required to put their property into a common stock. It was a voluntary matter. Nor is there an intimation in the New Testament that any church, except the one at Jerusalem, ever adopted the common-stock regulation. It was, doubtless, considered by that church a prudential arrangement, which involved temporary expediency rather than permanent principle. That the church at Antioch did not follow the example of the church at Jerusalem, in relation to this matter, is evident from Acts 11 : 29. " Then the disciples, every man according to his ability, determined to send relief to the brethren who dwelt in Judea." This *individual* determination shows that the property of the church was not in " common stock." And Paul's direction to the church at Corinth (1 Cor. 16 : 2) indicates that the Jerusalem policy had not been adopted. The same apostle too, in his letter to the Philippians, and to Timothy, refers to deacons. There was, therefore, a recognition of the deaconship when there was, so far as we know, no common property regulation. And more than this, the irresistible inference from Paul's first Epistle to Timothy, is that the office of deacon is as permanent as that of pastor. No one doubts that. the office of pastor is to be perpetuated to the end of time. The conclusion is that the deaconship is permanent in the churches of Christ, and that pastors and deacons are the only permanent Scriptural church officers.

The words—" men of honest report, full of the Holy Spirit, and wisdom "—applied to the first deacons, indicates that they were men of unblemished reputation, ardent piety, and good common sense. These qualifications should be sought in all who are appointed to the office of deacon. The phrase, " full of the Holy Spirit," is an admirable description of fervent, elevated piety; and in the selection of deacons their spirituality must be regarded, for their duties are not exclusively secular. Their secular duties, however, should be performed in a spiritual frame of mind; and in this way " they purchase to themselves a good degree, and obtain great boldness in the faith." In visiting the pious poor, to distribute the charities of the church, deacons must not perform the duty in a *formal* manner, but must inquire into the spiritual as well as the worldly circumstances of the recipients of the church's bounty. They will often witness such an exhibition of faith, patience, gratitude, and resignation as will richly repay them for their labor of love. As occasion may require, they should report to the pastor such cases as need his special attention, and thus they will become a connecting link between the pastor and the needy ones of the church.

As deacons were appointed at first " to serve tables," it may be well to say, there are three tables for them to serve: 1. *The table of the poor.* 2. *The table of the Lord.* 3. *The table of the pastor.* The pecuniary supplies to enable them to serve these tables must be furnished by the church. The custom of taking a collection for the poor when the Lord's Supper is administered is a good one, and worthy of universal adoption. It is suitable at the close of the solemn service to think of the pious poor, whom sickness or some other misfortune may have kept from the sacred feast.

As some pecuniary expenditure is necessary in furnishing the table of the Lord, this should be made through the deacons; and it is eminently proper, though not indispensable, for them to wait on the congregation in the distribution of the elements.

Deacons must serve the pastor's table. It is not for them to decide how liberally or scantily it shall be supplied. The church must make the decision, and enlarged views should be taken when it is made; for the energies of hundreds of pastors are greatly impaired by inadequate support.

In the twentieth century many churches employ other workers besides pastors. Problems related to church employees form a good example of what was earlier left to the deacons but now can best be handled another way. A church personnel committee serves well in formulating personnel policies and procedures for all employees, including the pastor.

As the work of modern churches grows in complexity, the need for a variety of standing committees should be studied. Many churches wait until a crisis develops and then take hasty action. How much better to have carefully chosen committees to study all areas of work. In this way many problems can be anticipated and dealt with by church action before they reach the crisis stage.

Good church committee work can have a major value in relation to the role of deacons. Without adequate committees, a church may leave its deacons to function as a kind of "fire department," calling on them to deal with whatever emergencies may develop. The church thus avoids planning, and it leaves the deacons to bear the brunt of its carelessness. Clearly, this is not fair to the deacons.

Instead of being "volunteer firemen" deacons should share with the pastor in the spiritual ministries of the church. Here is the role that is consistent with the place of the office in the New Testament. Deacons should be elected for specified terms, three years being typical. They should be chosen wisely in order to fill their role of spiritual leadership.

Ordaining deacons is a historic Baptist practice with New Testament precedent. At the beginning of his term, any deacon who has not been ordained should be, in accordance with Acts 6:6. Prayer, of course, is appropriate on all occasions, and laying on of hands is a token of designation to office. Some object to laying on of hands, supposing the design of this ceremony in apostolic times was the communication of the Holy Spirit. That the Spirit was sometimes given in connection with the imposition of hands is evident from Acts 8 : 17; but the first deacons were chosen because they were already " full of the Holy Spirit." Therefore the laying on of hands was not for the purpose of conferring the Holy Spirit, but of designating to office. This is the object of the ceremony now, and no one who has scriptural views supposes there is a bestowal of extraordinary gifts. It is the custom in some places to lay on hands in ordination during prayer. This is not according to scriptural example. Whenever prayer and laying on of hands are referred to in con-

nection with each other, as in Acts 6 : 6;
13 : 3, it is evident that prayer was *first* offered—then, followed imposition of hands—
to be seen and known as a designation to office, but which could not without a violation
of propriety be seen during prayer. It is very
desirable that all the churches adopt the practice of ordaining deacons by prayer and the
laying on of hands. It adds to the influence
of the deaconship when induction into it is
accompanied by appropriate services.

While pastors and deacons are the only
permanent scriptural church officers, it is a
prudential arrangement in all churches to
have a clerk; and owing to the requirements of
the civil law in some places, it is necessary to
have trustees. The business of the clerk of a
church is, of course, to keep a record of the
proceedings of the body. To secure accuracy
in the record, at every business meeting the
proceedings of the previous meeting should be
read, corrected (if correction is necessary), and
approved by the church. Trustees are generally the legal custodians of the church property, and are chosen by the church. They have
an official existence, because by civil statute it
is required that the legal right to property be

vested in individuals. It follows, therefore, that the manner of appointing trustees depends on the nature of the civil statute regulating the matter, and may be different in different states. In this area conforming with the requirements of state law is important. While most churches have never experienced legal difficulties, the possibility should not be ignored. Every church should be properly chartered and should select its trustees in line with the law. In any situation involving actual or potential court action, this is a valuable protection for the church.

The province of trustees is quite restricted. They have nothing to do with the spiritual affairs of the church. They cannot control the house of worship, saying how it shall be used, or who shall preach in it, and who shall not. The church must do all this. As church-members the trustees may with other members decide what shall be done with church property, whether the house of worship shall be sold and another built, etc., etc.; but *as trustees* they can do nothing in these matters. When the church so *orders,* they may convey or receive title to property, sue in the courts, etc., but their business as trustees is exclusively secular. They cannot in the capacity of trustees perform any spiritual function. A practical remembrance of this fact would have saved not a few churches from trouble.

It is said that in some churches the trustees fix the salaries of pastors; and from time to time increase or diminish them according to their pleasure—that they employ choirs, buy organs, engage sextons, etc., etc. All this is utterly indefensible. Trustees have not a particle of right to do these things. The government of a church is with its members. The churches must say what pastors' salaries shall be, whether music shall be led by choirs, with the aid of instruments or not, etc., etc. Nothing must be done which infringes the fundamental doctrine of church independence.

Trustees attend to the legal interests of the churches. They function in those matters where civil law specifically requires them to act in behalf of the church. Just as the pastor and the deacons are the spiritual officers of the church, the trustees are the legal officers. This does not mean that they make decisions about legal matters. It merely means that they meet the legal requirements for carrying out church decisions in matters involving law, such as buying or selling real estate. Since the function of trustees is so restricted, there appears to be no merit in the suggestion that trustees and deacons be combined. Such an idea is inconsistent with the spiritual function of the deacons.

CHAPTER III

THE phrase, *doctrines of a church,* is somewhat equivocal in its import. It may mean what a church teaches, or what a church believes the Bible to teach. It is here used in the latter sense. All who believe the Scriptures to be divinely inspired consider them the fountain of religious truth. The Bible contains the revelation of God to man. It is the supreme standard of faith and practice. Whatever conforms to this standard is right—whatever deviates from it is wrong. It is a duty incumbent upon all to " search the Scriptures " and learn what they teach. This duty cannot be faithfully performed unless prejudices and preconceived opinions are laid aside. Alas, how few study the Bible in this way. But for human imperfection there would doubtless be uniformity of belief as to what the Scriptures teach. There is not uniformity, but a deplorable variety of religious opinion throughout Christendom. Different sects, professing to take the word of God as their guide, contend as earnestly for their distinctive views as if they had different Bibles. Various constructions are placed on the teachings of the sacred volume, and multitudes of passages are diversely interpreted. Owing to this unfortunate fact, though belief of the Bible is significant as between the religionist and the infidel, it signifies nothing as between those who receive the Scriptures as the word of God. For they differ as to the import of the inspired Oracles; and *the meaning of the Bible is the Bible.* As there is such a diversity of opinion in the religious world, it is eminently proper for those who appeal to the Scriptures as the fountain of truth to declare what they believe the Scriptures to teach. To say that they believe the Scriptures is to say nothing to the purpose. All will say this, and yet all differ as to the teachings of the Bible. There must be some distinctive declaration. What a man believes the Bible to teach is his Creed, either written or unwritten. And though it has sometimes been said that creeds have produced differences of religious opinion, it would be nearer to the truth, logically and historically, to say that differences of religious opinion have produced creeds.

As to declarations of faith, it must ever be understood that they are not substitutes for the Scriptures. They are only exponents of what are conceived to be the fundamental doctrines of the word of God. Among Baptists, as their churches are independent, it is optional with each church to have a declaration or not, as it may think best. Each church too may adopt a declaration of its own. Its independence gives it this right, nor can it be alienated. While Baptists glory in their form of church government—which recognizes every church as a little republic in itself—they are perhaps as nearly united in their views of the truths of the Bible as most other denominations. The following Declaration of Faith expresses, substantially, what Baptists believe concerning the topics mentioned.[1]

DECLARATION OF FAITH

I. OF THE SCRIPTURES

We believe that the Holy Bible was written by men divinely inspired, and is a perfect treasure of

[1] See page 178 for further information about Baptist declarations of faith.

heavenly instruction;[1] that it has God for its author, salvation for its end,[2] and truth without any mixture of error for its matter;[3] that it reveals the principles by which God will judge us;[4] and therefore is, and shall remain to the end of the world, the true center of Christian union,[5] and the supreme standard by which all human conduct, creeds, and opinions should be tried.[6]

Places in the Bible where taught.

[1] 2 Tim. 3 : 16, 17. All Scripture is given by inspiration of God, and is profitable for doctrine, for reproof, for correction, for instruction in righteousness; that the man of God may be perfect, thoroughly furnished unto all good works. Also 2 Peter 1 : 21; 2 Sam. 23 : 2; Acts 1 : 16; 3 : 21; John 10 : 35; Luke 16 : 29-31; Ps. 119 : 111; Rom. 3 : 1, 2.

[2] 2 Tim. 3 : 15,—able to make thee wise unto salvation. Also 1 Peter 1 : 10-12; Acts 11 : 14; Rom. 1 : 16; Mark 16 : 16; John 5 : 38, 39.

[3] Prov. 30 : 5, 6. Every word of God is pure,—Add thou not unto his words, lest he reprove thee, and thou be found a liar. Also John 17 : 17; Rev. 22 : 18, 19; Rom. 3 : 4.

[4] Rom. 2 : 12. As many as have sinned in the law, shall be judged by the law. John 12 : 47, 48. If any man hear my words—the word that I have spoken—the same shall judge him in the last day. Also 1 Cor. 4 : 3, 4. Luke 10 : 10-16; 12 : 47, 48.

[5] Phil. 3 : 16. Let us walk in the same rule; let us mind the same thing. Also Eph. 4 : 3-6; Phil. 2 : 1, 2; 1 Cor. 1 : 10; 1 Peter 4 : 11.

[6] 1 John 4 : 1. Beloved, believe not every spirit, but try the spirits whether they are of God. Isa. 8 : 20. To the law and to the testimony; if they speak not according to this word, it is because there is no light in them. 1 Thess. 5 : 21. Prove all things. 2 Cor. 13 : 5. Prove your own selves. Also Acts 17 : 11: 1 John 4 : 6; Jude 3 : 5; Eph. 6 : 17; Ps. 119 : 59, 60; Phil. 1 : 9-11.

II. OF THE TRUE GOD

We believe that there is one, and only one living and true God, an infinite, intelligent Spirit, whose name is JEHOVAH, the Maker and Supreme Ruler of heaven and earth;[1] inexpressibly glorious in holiness,[2] and worthy of all possible honor, confidence, and love;[3] that in the unity of the Godhead there are three persons, the Father, the Son, and the Holy Ghost;[4] equal in every divine perfection,[5] and executing distinct but harmonious offices in the great work of redemption[6]

Places in the Bible where taught.

[1] John 4 : 24. God is a Spirit. Ps. 147 : 5. His understanding is infinite. Ps. 83 : 18. Thou whose name alone is JEHOVAH, art the Most High over all the earth. Heb. 3 : 4; Rom. 1 : 20; Jer. 10 : 10.

[2] Exod. 15 : 11. Who is like unto Thee—glorious in holiness? Isa. 6 : 3; 1 Peter 1 : 15, 16; Rev. 4 : 6-8.

[3] Mark 12 : 30. Thou shalt love the Lord thy God with all thy heart, and with all thy soul, and with all thy mind, and with all thy strength. Rev. 4 : 11. Thou art worthy, O Lord, to receive glory, and honor, and power: for thou hast created all things, and for thy pleasure they are and were created. Matt. 10 : 37; Jer. 2 : 12, 13.

[4] Matt. 28 : 19. Go ye therefore and teach all nations, baptizing them in the name of the Father, and of the Son, and of the Holy Ghost. John 15 : 26. When the Comforter is come, whom I will send you from the Father, even the Spirit of Truth, which proceedeth from the Father, he shall testify of me. 1 Cor. 12 : 4-6. 1 John 5 : 7.

[5] John 10 : 30. I and my Father are one. John 5 : 17; 14 : 23; 17 : 5, 10; Acts 5 : 3, 4; 1 Cor. 2 : 10, 11; Phil. 2 : 5, 6.

[6] Eph. 2 : 18. For through Him [the Son] we both have an access by one Spirit unto the Father. 2 Cor. 13 : 14. The grace of our Lord Jesus Christ, and the love of God, and the communion of the Holy Ghost, be with you all. Rev. 1 : 4, 5. Comp. 2 : 7.

III. OF THE FALL OF MAN

We believe that man was created in holiness, under the law of his Maker;[1] but by voluntary transgression fell from that holy and happy state;[2] in consequence of which all mankind are now sinners,[3] not by constraint but choice;[4] being by nature utterly void of that holiness required by the law of God, positively inclined to evil; and therefore under just condemnation to eternal ruin,[5] without defence or excuse.[6]

Places in the Bible where taught.

[1] Gen. 1 : 27. God created man in his own image. Gen. 1 : 31. And God saw every thing that he had made, and behold, it was very good. Eccl. 7 : 29; Acts 15 : 26; Gen. 2 : 16.

[2] Gen. 3 : 6-24. And when the woman saw that the tree was good for food, and that it was pleasant to the eyes, and a tree to be desired to make one wise; she took of the fruit thereof, and did eat; and gave unto her husband with her, and he did eat. Therefore the Lord God drove out the man; and he placed at the east of the garden of Eden, Cherubim, and a flaming sword which turned every way to keep the way of the tree of life. Rom. 5 : 12.

[3] Rom. 5 : 19. By one man's disobedience many were made sinners. John 3 : 6; Ps. 51 : 5; Rom. 5 : 15-19; 8 : 7.

[4] Isa. 53 : 6. We have turned, every one to his own way. Gen. 6 : 12; Rom. 3 : 9-18.

[5] Eph. 2 : 1-3. Among whom also we all had our conversation in times past in the lusts of our flesh, fulfilling the desires of the flesh and of the mind; and were by nature the children of wrath even as others. Rom. 1 : 18. For the wrath of God is revealed from heaven against all ungodliness and unrighteousness of men, who hold the truth in unrighteousness. Rom. 1 : 32; 2 : 1-16; Gal. 3 : 10; Matt. 20 : 15.

[6] Ezek. 18 : 19, 20. Yet say ye, Why? doth not the son bear the iniquity of the father?—the soul that sinneth it shall die. The son shall not bear the iniquity of the father, neither shall the father bear the iniquity of the son; the righteousness of

the righteous shall be upon him, and the wickedness of the wicked shall be upon him. Rom. 1 : 20. So that they are without excuse. Rom. 3 : 19. That every mouth may be stopped and all the world may become guilty before God. Gal. 3 : 22.

IV. OF THE WAY OF SALVATION

We believe that the salvation of sinners is wholly of grace;[1] through the Mediatorial offices of the Son of God;[2] who by the appointment of the Father, freely took upon him our nature, yet without sin;[3] honored the divine law by his personal obedience,[4] and by his death made a full atonement for our sins;[5] that having risen from the dead, he is now enthroned in heaven;[6] and uniting in his wonderful person the tenderest sympathies with divine perfections, he is every way qualified to be a suitable, a compassionate, and an all-sufficient Saviour.[7]

Places in the Bible where taught.

[1] Eph. 2 : 5. By grace ye are saved. Matt. 18 : 11; 1 John 4 : 10; 1 Cor. 3 : 5-7; Acts 15 : 11.

[2] John 3 : 16. For God so loved the world that he gave his only begotten Son, that whosoever believeth in him should not perish, but have everlasting life. John 1 : 1-14; Heb. 4 : 14; 12 : 24.

[3] Phil. 2 : 6, 7. Who being in the form of God, thought it not robbery to be equal with God; but made himself of no reputation, and took upon him the form of a servant, and was made in the likeness of men. Heb. 2 : 9, 14; 2 Cor. 5 : 21.

[4] Isa. 42 : 21. The Lord is well pleased for his righteousness' sake; he will magnify the law and make it honorable. Phil. 2 : 8; Gal. 4 : 4, 5; Rom. 3 : 21.

[5] Isa. 53 : 4, 5. He was wounded for our transgressions, he was bruised for our iniquities; the chastisement of our peace was upon him; and with his stripes we are healed. Matt. 20 : 28; Rom. 4 : 25; 3 : 21-26; 1 John 4 : 10; 2 : 3; 1 Cor. 15 : 1-3; Heb. 9 : 13-15.

[6] Heb. 1 : 8. Unto the Son he saith, thy throne, O God, is for ever and ever. Heb. 1 : 3; 8 : 1; Col. 3 : 1-4.

[7] Heb. 7 : 25. Wherefore he is able also to save them to the uttermost that come unto God by him, seeing he ever liveth to make intercession for them. Col. 2 : 9. For in him dwelleth all the fullness of the Godhead bodily. Heb. 2 : 18. In that he himself hath suffered, being tempted, he is able to succor them that are tempted. Heb. 7 : 26; Ps. 89 : 19; Ps. 45.

V. OF JUSTIFICATION

We believe that the great gospel blessing which Christ[1] secures to such as believe in him is justification;[2] that justification includes the pardon of sin,[3] and the promise of eternal life on principles of righteousness;[4] that it is bestowed, not in consideration of any works of righteousness which we have done, but solely through faith in the Redeemer's blood;[5] by virtue of which faith his perfect righteousness is freely imputed to us of God;[6] that it brings us into a state of most blessed peace and favor with God, and secures every other blessing needful for time and eternity.[7]

Places in the Bible where taught.

[1] John 1 : 16. Of his fullness have all we received. Eph. 3 : 8.

[2] Acts 13 : 39. By him all that believe are justified from all things. Isa. 3 : 11, 12; Rom. 8 : 1.

[3] Rom. 5 : 9. Being justified by his blood, we shall be saved from wrath through him. Zech. 13 : 1; Matt. 9 : 6; Acts 10 : 43.

[4] Rom. 5 : 17. They which receive the abundance of grace and of the gift of righteousness shall reign in life by one, Jesus Christ. Titus 3 : 5, 6; 1 Peter 3 : 7; 1 John 2 : 25; Rom. 5 : 21.

[5] Rom. 4 : 4, 5. Now to him that worketh is the reward not reckoned of grace, but of debt. But to him that worketh not, but believeth on him that justifieth the ungodly, his faith is counted for righteousness. Rom. 5 : 21; 6 : 23; Phil. 3 : 7-9.

[6] Rom. 5 : 19. By the obedience of one shall many be made righteous. Rom. 3 : 24-28; 4 : 23-25; 1 John 2 : 12.

[7] Rom. 5 : 1, 2. Being justified by faith, we have peace with God, through our Lord Jesus Christ; by whom also we have access·by faith into this grace wherein we stand and rejoice in hope of the glory of God. Rom. 5 : 3. We glory in tribulations also. Rom. 5 : 11. We also joy in God. 1 Cor. 1 : 30, 31; Matt. 6 : 33; 1 Tim. 4 : 8.

VI. OF THE FREENESS OF SALVATION

We believe that the blessings of salvation are made free to all by the gospel;[1] that it is the immediate duty of all to accept them by a cordial penitent and obedient faith;[2] and that nothing prevents the salvation of the greatest sinner on earth, but his own inherent depravity and voluntary rejection of the gospel;[3] which rejection involves him in an aggravated condemnation.[4]

Places in the Bible where taught.

[1] Isa. 55 : 1. Ho, every one that thirsteth, come ye to the waters. Rev. 22 : 17. Whosoever will, let him take the water of life freely. Luke 14 : 17.

[2] Rom. 16 : 26. The gospel—according to the commandment of the everlasting God, made known to all nations for the obedience of faith. Mark 1 : 15. Rom. 1 : 15-17.

[3] John 5 : 40. Ye will not come to me, that ye might have life. Matt. 23 : 37; Rom. 9 : 32; Prov. 1 : 24; Acts 13 : 46.

[4] John 3 : 19. And this is the condemnation, that light is come into the world, and men loved darkness rather than light because their deeds were evil. Matt. 11 : 20; Luke 19 : 27; 2 Thess. 1 : 8.

VII. OF GRACE IN REGENERATION

We believe that in order to be saved, sinners must be regenerated, or born again;[1] that regeneration consists in giving a holy disposition to the mind;[2]

that it is effected in a manner above our comprehension by the power of the Holy Spirit, in connection with divine truth,[3] so as to secure our voluntary obedience to the gospel;[4] and that its proper evidence appears in the holy fruits of repentance, and faith, and newness of life.[5]

Places in the Bible where taught.

[1] John 3 : 3. Verily, verily, I say unto thee, except a man be born again, he cannot see the kingdom of God. John 3 : 6, 7; 1 Cor. 1 : 14; Rev. 8 : 7-9; 21 : 27.

[2] 2 Cor. 5 : 17. If any man be in Christ, he is a new creature. Ezek. 36 : 26; Deut. 30 : 6; Rom. 2 : 28, 29; 5 : 5; 1 John 4 : 7.

[3] John 3 . 8. The wind bloweth where it listeth, and thou hearest the sound thereof, but canst not tell whence it cometh and whither it goeth; so is every one that is born of the Spirit. John 1 : 13. Which were born, not of blood, nor of the will of the flesh, nor of the will of man, but of God. James 1 : 16-18. Of his own will begat he us with the word of truth. 1 Cor. 1 : 30; Phil. 2 : 13.

[4] 1 Peter 1 : 22-25. Ye have purified your souls by obeying the truth through the Spirit. 1 John 5 : 1. Whosoever believeth that Jesus is the Christ is born of God. Eph. 4 : 20-24; Col. 3 : 9-11.

[5] Eph. 5 : 9. The fruit of the Spirit is in all goodness, and righteousness and truth. Rom. 8 : 9; Gal. 5 : 16-23; Eph. 3 : 14-21; Matt. 3 : 8-10; 7 : 20; 1 John 5 : 4, 18.

VIII. OF REPENTANCE AND FAITH

We believe that repentance and faith are sacred duties, and also inseparable graces, wrought in our souls by the regenerating Spirit of God;[1] whereby being deeply convinced of our guilt, danger, and helplessness, and of the way of salvation by Christ,[2] we turn to God with unfeigned contrition, confession, and supplication for mercy;[3] at the same time heartily receiving the Lord Jesus Christ as our Prophet, Priest, and King, and relying on him alone as the only and all-sufficient Saviour.[4]

Places in the Bible where taught.

[1] Mark 1 : 15. Repent ye, and believe the gospel. Acts 11 : 18. Then hath God also to the Gentiles granted repentance unto life. Eph. 2 : 8. By grace ye are saved, through faith; and that not of yourselves; it is the gift of God. 1 John 5 : 1. Whosoever believeth that Jesus is the Christ is born of God.

[2] John 16 : 8. He will reprove the world of sin, and of righteousness, and of judgment. Acts 2 : 37, 38. They were pricked in their heart, and said—Men and brethren, what shall we do? Then Peter said unto them, Repent, and be baptized every one of you in the name of Jesus Christ for the remission of your sins. Acts 16 : 30, 31.

[3] Luke 18 : 13. And the publican—smote upon his breast, saying, God be merciful to me a sinner. Luke 15 : 18-21; James 4 : 7-10; 2 Cor. 7 : 11; Rom. 10 : 12, 13; Ps. 51.

[4] Rom. 10 : 9-11. If thou shalt confess with thy mouth the Lord Jesus, and shalt believe in thy heart that God hath raised him from the dead, thou shalt be saved. Acts 3 : 22, 23; Heb. 5 : 14; Ps. 2 : 6; Heb. 1 : 8; 8 : 25; 2 Tim. 1 : 12.

IX. OF GOD'S PURPOSE OF GRACE

We believe that election is the eternal purpose of God, according to which he graciously regenerates, sanctifies, and saves sinners;[1] that being perfectly consistent with the free agency of man, it comprehends all the means in connection with the end;[2] that it is a most glorious display of God's sovereign goodness, being infinitely free, wise, holy, and unchangeable;[3] that it utterly excludes boasting, and promotes humility, love, prayer, praise, trust in God, and active imitation of his free mercy;[4] that it encourages the use of means in the highest degree;[5] that it may be ascertained by its effects in all who truly believe the gospel;⁶ that it is the foundation of Christian assurance;⁷ and that to ascertain it with regard to ourselves demands and deserves the utmost diligence.⁸

Places in the Bible where taught.

¹ 2 Tim. 1 : 8, 9. Be not thou therefore ashamed of the testimony of our Lord, nor of me his prisoner; but be thou partaker of the afflictions of the gospel, according to the power of God; who hath saved us and called us with an holy calling, not according to our works, but according to his own purpose and grace, which was given us in Christ Jesus before the world began. Eph. 1 : 3-14; 1 Peter 1 : 1, 2; Rom. 11 : 5, 6; John 15 : 16; 1 John 4 : 19; Hosea 12 : 9.

² 2 Thess. 2 : 13, 14. But we are bound to give thanks always to God for you, brethren beloved of the Lord, because God hath from the beginning chosen you to salvation, through sanctification of the Spirit, and belief of the truth; whereunto he called you by our gospel, to the obtaining of the glory of our Lord Jesus Christ. Acts 13 : 48; John 10 : 16; Matt. 20 : 16; Acts 15 : 14.

³ Exod. 33 : 18, 19. And Moses said, I beseech thee, show me thy glory. And he said, I will cause all my goodness to pass before thee, and I will proclaim the name of the Lord before thee, and will be gracious to whom I will be gracious, and will show mercy on whom I will show mercy. Matt. 20 : 15. Is it not lawful for me to do what I will with my own? Is thine eye evil because I am good? Eph. 1 : 11; Rom. 9 : 23, 24; Jer. 31 : 3; Rom. 11 : 28, 29; James 1 : 17, 18; 2 Tim. 1 : 9; Rom. 11 : 32-36.

⁴ 1 Cor. 4 : 7. For who maketh thee to differ from another? and what hast thou that thou didst not receive? Now if thou didst receive it, why dost thou glory as if thou hadst not received it? 1 Cor. 1 : 26-31; Rom. 3 : 27; 4 : 16; Col. 3 : 12; 1 Cor. 3 : 5-7; 15 : 10; 1 Peter 5 : 10; Acts 1 : 24; 1 Thess. 2 : 13; 1 Peter 2 : 9; Luke 18 : 7; John 15 : 16; Eph. 1 : 16; 1 Thess. 2 : 12.

⁵ 2 Tim. 2 : 10. Therefore I endure all things for the elects' sake, that they also may obtain the salvation which is in Christ Jesus with eternal glory. 1 Cor. 9 : 22. I am made all things to all men, that I might by all means save some. Rom. 8 : 28-30; John 6 : 37-40; 2 Peter 1 : 10.

[6] 1 Thess. 1 : 4-10. Knowing, brethren beloved, your election of God; for our gospel came unto you, not in word only, but in power, and in the Holy Ghost, and in much assurance, etc.

[7] Rom. 8 : 28-31. Moreover, whom he did predestinate, them he also called, and whom he called them he also justified, and whom he justified them he also glorified. What shall we then say to these things? If God be for us, who can be against us? Isa. 42 : 16; Rom. 11 : 29.

[8] 2 Peter 1 : 10, 11. Wherefore the rather, brethren, give diligence to make your calling and election sure; for if ye do these things, ye shall never fall; for so an entrance shall be ministered unto you abundantly into the everlasting kingdom of our Lord and Saviour Jesus Christ. Phil. 3 : 12; Heb. 6 : 11.

X. OF SANCTIFICATION

We believe that sanctification is the process by which, according to the will of God, we are made partakers of his holiness;[1] that it is a progressive work;[2] that it is begun in regeneration;[3] and that it is carried on in the hearts of believers by the presence and power of the Holy Spirit, the Sealer and Comforter, in the continual use of the appointed means—especially, the word of God, self-examination, self-denial, watchfulness, and prayer.[4]

Places in the Bible where taught.

[1] Thess. 4 : 3. For this is the will of God, even your sanctification. 1 Thess. 5 : 23. And the very God of peace sanctify you wholly. 2 Cor. 7 : 1; 13 : 9; Eph. 1 : 4.

[2] Prov. 4 : 18. The path of the just is as the shining light which shineth more and more unto the perfect day. 2 Cor. 3 : 18; Heb. 6 : 1; 2 Peter 1 : 5-8; Phil. 3 : 12-16.

[3] John 2 : 29. If ye know that he [God] is righteous, ye know that every one that doeth righteousness is born of him. Rom. 8 : 5. They that are after the flesh, do mind the things of the flesh; but they that are after the Spirit the things of the Spirit. John 3 : 6; Phil. 1 : 9-11; Eph. 1 : 13, 14.

[4] Phil. 2 : 12, 13. Work out your own salvation with fear and trembling, for it is God which worketh in you both to will

and to do, of his good pleasure. Eph. 4 : 11, 12; 1 Peter 2 : 2; 2 Peter 3 : 18; 2 Cor. 13 : 5; Luke 11 : 35; 9 : 23; Matt. 26 : 41; Eph. 6 : 18; 4 : 30.

XI. OF THE PERSEVERANCE OF SAINTS

We believe that such only are real believers as endure unto the end;[1] that their persevering attachment to Christ is the grand mark which distinguishes them from superficial professors;[2] that a special providence watches over their welfare,[3] and that they are kept by the power of God through faith unto salvation.[4]

Places in the Bible where taught.

[1] John 8 : 31. Then said Jesus—If ye continue in my word, then are ye my disciples indeed. 1 John 2 : 27, 28; 3 : 9; 5 : 18.

[2] 1 John 2 : 19. They went out from us, but they were not of us; for if they had been of us, they would no doubt have continued with us; but they went out that it might be made manifest that they were not all of us. John 13 : 18; Matt. 13 : 20, 21; John 6 : 66-69; Job 17 : 9.

[3] Rom. 8 : 28. And we know that all things work together for good unto them that love God, to them who are the called according to his purpose. Matt. 6 : 30-33; Jer. 32 : 40; Ps. 121 : 3; 91 : 11, 12.

[4] Phil. 1 : 6. He who hath begun a good work in you, will perform it until the day of Jesus Christ. Phil. 2 : 12, 13; Jude 24, 25; Heb. 1 : 14; 2 Kings 6 : 16; Heb. 13 : 5; 1 John 4 : 4.

XII. OF THE HARMONY OF THE LAW AND THE GOSPEL

We believe that the law of God is the eternal and unchangeable rule of his moral government;[1] that it is holy, just, and good;[2] and that the inability which the Scriptures ascribe to fallen men to fulfill its precepts, arises entirely from their love of sin:[2] to deliver them from which, and to restore them through a Mediator to unfeigned obedience to the holy law, is one great end of the gospel, and of the means of grace connected with the establishment of the visible church.[4]

Places in the Bible where taught.

[1] Rom. 3 : 31. Do we make void the law through faith? God forbid. Yea, we establish the law. Matt. 5 : 17; Luke 16 : 17; Rom. 3 : 20; 4 : 15.

[2] Rom. 7 : 12. The law is holy, and the commandment holy, and just, and good. Rom. 7 : 7, 14, 22; Gal. 3 : 21; Ps. 119.

[3] Rom. 8 : 7, 8. The carnal mind is enmity against God, for it is not subject to the law of God, neither indeed can be. So then they that are in the flesh cannot please God. Josh. 24 : 19; Jer. 13 : 23; John 6 : 44; 5 : 44.

[4] Rom. 8 : 2, 4. For the law of the spirit of Life in Christ Jesus hath made me free from the law of sin and death. For what the law could not do, in that it was weak through the flesh, God, sending his own Son in the likeness of sinful flesh, and for sin, condemned sin in the flesh; that the righteousness of the law might be fulfilled in us, who walk not after the flesh but after the Spirit. Rom. 10 : 4; 1 Tim. 1 : 5; Heb. 8 : 10; Jude 20, 21; Heb. 12 : 14; Matt. 16 : 17, 18; 1 Cor. 12 : 28.

XIII. OF A GOSPEL CHURCH

We believe that a visible church of Christ is a congregation of baptized believers,[1] associated by covenant in the faith and fellowship of the gospel;[2] observing the ordinances of Christ;[3] governed by his laws;[4] and exercising the gifts, rights, and privileges invested in them by his word;[5] that its only scriptural officers are bishops or pastors and deacons,[6] whose qualifications, claims, and duties are defined in the Epistles to Timothy and Titus.

Places in the Bible where taught.

[1] 1 Cor. 1 : 1-13. Paul—unto the church of God which is at Corinth. Is Christ divided? Was Paul crucified for you? Or were ye baptized in the name of Paul? Matt. 18 : 17; Acts 5 : 11; 8 : 1; 11 : 31; 1 Cor. 4 : 17; 14 : 23; 3 John 9; 1 Tim. 3 : 5.

[2] Acts 2 : 41, 42. Then they that gladly received his word were baptized; and the same day there were added to them about three thousand souls. 2 Cor. 8 : 5. They first gave their ownselves to the Lord, and unto us by the will of God. Acts 2 : 47; 1 Cor. 5 : 12, 13.

[3] 1 Cor. 11 : 2. Now I praise you, brethren, that ye remember me in all things, and keep the ordinances as I delivered them unto you. 2 Thess. 3 : 6; Rom. 16 : 17-20; 1 Cor. 11 : 23; Matt. 18 : 15-20; 1 Cor. 5 : 6; 2 Cor. 2 : 7; 1 Cor. 4 : 11.

[4] Matt. 28 : 20. Teaching them to observe all things whatsoever I have commanded you. John 14 : 15; 15 : 12; 1 John 4 : 21; John 14 : 21; 1 Thess. 4 : 2; 2 John 6; Gal. 6 : 2. All the Epistles.

[5] Eph. 4 : 7. Unto every one of us is given grace according to the measure of the gift of Christ. 1 Cor. 14 : 12. Seek that ye may excel to the edifying of the church. Phil. 1 : 27. That I may hear of your affairs, that ye stand fast in one spirit, with one mind, striving together for the faith of the gospel. 1 Cor. 12 : 14.

[6] Phil. 1 : 1. With the bishops and deacons. Acts 14 : 23; 15 : 22; 1 Tim. 3; Titus 1.

XIV. OF BAPTISM AND THE LORD'S SUPPER

We believe that Christian baptism is the immersion in water of a believer,[1] into the name of the Father, and Son, and Holy Ghost:[2] to show forth in a solemn and beautiful emblem, our faith in the crucified, buried, and risen Saviour, with its effect, in our death to sin and resurrection to a new life;[3] that it is prerequisite to the privileges of a church relation; and to the Lord's Supper,[4] in which the members of the church by the sacred use of bread and wine, are to commemorate together the dying love of Christ;[5] preceded always by solemn self-examination.[6]

Places in the Bible where taught.

[1] Acts 8 : 36-39. And the eunuch said, See, here is water what doth hinder me to be baptized? And Philip said, If thou believest with all thy heart thou mayest. And they went down into the water, both Philip and the eunuch, and he baptized him. Matt. 3 : 5, 6; John 3 : 22, 23; 4 : 1, 2; Matt. 28 : 19; Mark 16 : 16; Acts 2 : 38; 8 : 12; 16 : 32-34; 18 : 8.

[2] Matt. 28 : 19. Baptizing them in the name of the Father, and of the Son, and of the Holy Ghost. Acts 10 : 47, 48; Gal. 3 : 27, 28.

[3] Rom. 6 : 4. Therefore we are buried with him by baptism into death; that like as Christ was raised from the dead by the glory of the Father, even so we also should walk in newness of life. Col. 2 : 12; 1 Pet. 3 : 20, 21; Acts 22 : 16.

[4] Acts 2 : 41, 42. Then they that gladly received his word were baptized, and there were added to them, the same day, about three thousand souls. And they continued steadfastly in the Apostles' doctrine and fellowship, and in breaking of bread, and in prayers. Matt. 28 : 19, 20. Acts and Epistles.

[5] 1 Cor. 11 : 26. As often as ye eat this bread and drink this cup, ye do show the Lord's death till he come. Matt. 26 : 26-29; Mark 14 : 22-25; Luke 22 : 14-20.

[6] 1 Cor. 11 : 28. But let a man examine himself, and so let him eat of that bread and drink of that cup. 1 Cor. 5 : 1, 8; 10 : 3-32; 11 : 17-32; John 6 : 26-71.

XV. OF THE CHRISTIAN SABBATH

We believe that the first day of the week is the Lord's Day, or Christian Sabbath;[1] and is to be kept sacred to religious purposes,[2] by abstaining from all secular labor and sinful recreations,[3] by the devout observance of all the means of grace, both private[4] and public;[5] and by preparation for that rest that remaineth for the people of God.[6]

Places in the Bible where taught.

[1] Acts 20 : 7. On the first day of the week, when the disciples came together to break bread, Paul preached to them. Gen. 2 : 3; Col. 2 : 16, 17; Mark 2 : 27; John 20 : 19; 1 Cor. 16 : 1, 2.

[2] Exod. 20 : 8. Remember the Sabbath Day, to keep it holy. Rev. 1 : 10. I was in the Spirit on the Lord's Day. Ps. 118 : 24. This is the day which the Lord hath made: we will rejoice and be glad in it.

[3] Isa. 58 : 13, 14. If thou turn away thy foot from the Sabbath, from doing thy pleasure on my holy day; and call the Sabbath a delight, the holy of the Lord honorable; and shalt honor him, not doing thine own ways, nor finding thine own pleasure, nor speaking thine own words; then shalt thou delight thyself in the Lord, and I will cause thee to ride upon the high places of the earth, and feed thee with the heritage of Jacob. Isa. 56 : 2-8.

[4] Ps. 118 : 15. The voice of rejoicing and salvation is in the tabernacles of the righteous.

[5] Heb. 10 : 24, 25. Not forsaking the assembling of yourselves together, as the manner of some is. Acts 11 : 26. A whole year they assembled themselves with the church, and taught much people. Acts 13 : 44. The next sabbath day came almost the whole city together to hear the word of God. Lev. 19 : 30; Exod. 46 : 3; Luke 4 : 16; Acts 17 : 2, 3; Ps. 26 : 8; 87 : 3.

[6] Heb. 4 : 3-11. Let us labor therefore to enter into that rest.

XVI. OF CIVIL GOVERNMENT

We believe that civil government is of divine appointment, for the interests and good order of human society;[1] and that magistrates are to be prayed for, conscientiously honored, and obeyed;[2] except only in things opposed to the will of our Lord Jesus Christ,[3] who is the only Lord of the conscience, and the Prince of the kings of the earth.[4]

Places in the Bible where taught.

[1] Rom. 13 : 1-7. The powers that be are ordained of God. For rulers are not a terror to good works, but to the evil. Deut. 16 : 18; 2 Sam. 23 : 3; Exod. 18 : 23; Jer. 30 : 21.

[2] Matt. 22 : 21. Render therefore unto Cæsar the things that are Cæsar's, and unto God the things that are God's. Titus 3 : 1; 1 Peter 2 : 13; 1 Tim. 2 : 1-8.

[3] Acts 5 : 29. We ought to obey God rather than man. Matt. 10 : 28. Fear not them which kill the body, but are not able to kill the soul. Dan. 3 : 15-18; 6 : 7-10; Acts 4 : 18-20.

[4] Matt. 23 : 10. Ye have one Master, even Christ. Rom. 14 : 4. Who art thou that judgest another man's servant? Rev. 19 : 16. And he hath on his vesture and on his thigh a name written, KING OF KINGS, AND LORD OF LORDS. Ps. 72 : 11; Ps. 2; Rom. 14 : 9-13.

XVII. OF THE RIGHTEOUS AND THE WICKED

We believe that there is a radical and essential difference between the righteous and the wicked;[1] that such only as through faith are justified in the name of the Lord Jesus, and sanctified by the Spirit of our God, are truly righteous in his esteem;[2] while all such as continue in impenitence and unbelief are in his sight wicked, and under the curse;[3] and this distinction holds among men both in and after death.[4]

Places in the Bible where taught.

[1] Mal. 3 : 18. Ye shall discern between the righteous and the wicked; between him that serveth God and him that serveth him not. Prov. 12 : 26; Isa. 5 : 20; Gen. 18 : 23; Jer. 15 : 19; Acts 10 : 34, 35; Rom. 6 : 16.

[2] Rom. 1 : 17. The just shall live by faith. Rom. 7 : 6. We are delivered from the law, that being dead wherein we were held, that we should serve in newness of spirit, and not in the oldness of the letter. 1 John 2 : 29. If ye know that he is righteous, ye know that every one that doeth righteousness is born of him. 1 John 3 : 7; Rom. 6 : 18, 22; 1 Cor. 11 : 32; Prov. 11 : 31; 1 Peter 4 : 17, 18.

[8] 1 John 5 : 19. And we know that we are of God, and the whole world lieth in wickedness. Gal. 3 : 10. As many as are of the works of the law, are under the curse. John 3 : 36; Isa. 57 : 21; Ps. 10 : 4; Isa. 55 : 6, 7.

[4] Prov. 14 : 32. The wicked is driven away in his wickedness, but the righteousness hath hope in his death. See also the example of the rich man and Lazarus. Luke 16 : 25. Thou in thy lifetime receivedst thy good things, and likewise Lazarus evil things: but now he is comforted, and thou art tormented. John 8 : 21-24; Prov. 10 : 24; Luke 12 : 4, 5; 9 : 23-26; John 12 : 25, 26; Eccl. 3 : 17; Matt. 13, 14.

XVIII. OF THE WORLD TO COME

We believe that the end of this world is approaching;[1] that at the Last Day Christ will descend from heaven,[2] and raise the dead from the grave to final retribution;[3] that a solemn separation will then take place;[4] that the wicked will be adjudged to endless punishment, and the righteous to endless joy;[5] and that this judgment will fix forever the final state of men in heaven or hell, on principles of righteousness.[6]

Places in the Bible where taught.

[1] 1 Pet. 4 : 7. But the end of all things is at hand; be ye therefore sober, and watch unto prayer. 1 Cor. 7 : 29-31; Heb. 1 : 10-12; Matt. 24 : 35; 1 John 2 : 17; Matt. 28 : 20; 13 : 39, 40; 2 Peter 3 : 3-13.

[2] Acts 1 : 11. This same Jesus which is taken up from you into heaven, shall so come in like manner as ye have seen him go into heaven. Rev. 1 : 7; Heb. 9 : 28; Acts 3 : 21; 1 Thess. 4 : 13-18; 5 : 1-11.

[3] Acts 24 : 15. There shall be a resurrection of the dead, both of the just and unjust. 1 Cor. 15 : 12-59; Luke 14 : 14; Dan. 12 : 2; John 5 : 28, 29; 6 : 40; 11 : 25, 26; 2 Tim. 1 : 10; Acts 10 : 42.

[4] Matt. 13 : 49. The angels shall come forth and sever the wicked from among the just. Matt. 13 : 37-43; 24 : 30, 31; 25 : 31-33.

⁸ Matt. 25 : 35-41. And these shall go away into everlasting punishment, but the righteous into life eternal. Rev. 22 : 11. He that is unjust, let him be unjust still; and he which is filthy, let him be filthy still; and he that is righteous, let him be righteous still; and he that is holy, let him be holy still. 1 Cor. 6 : 9, 10; Mark 9 : 43-48; 2 Peter 2 : 9; Jude 7; Phil. 3 : 19; Rom. 6 : 22; 2 Cor. 5 : 10, 11; John 4 : 36; 2 Cor. 4 : 18.

⁶ Rom. 3 : 5, 6. Is God unrighteous, who taketh vengeance? (I speak as a man.) God forbid; for how then shall God judge the world? 2 Thess. 1 : 6-12. Seeing it is a righteous thing with God to recompense tribulation to them that trouble you, and to you who are troubled, rest with us—when he shall come to be glorified in his saints and to be admired in all them that believe. Heb. 6 : 1, 2; 1 Cor. 4 : 5; Acts 17 : 31; Rom. 2 : 2-16; Rev. 20 : 11, 12; 1 John 2 : 28; 4 : 17.

SEEING THEN THAT ALL THESE THINGS SHALL BE DISSOLVED, WHAT MANNER OF PERSONS OUGHT YE TO BE IN ALL HOLY CONVERSATION AND GODLINESS, LOOKING FOR AND HASTING UNTO THE COMING OF THE DAY OF GOD? 2 Peter 3 : 11, 12.

CHURCH COVENANT

Having been led, as we believe, by the Spirit of God, to receive the Lord Jesus Christ as our Saviour, and on the profession of our faith, having been baptized in the name of the Father, and of the Son, and of the Holy Ghost, we do now in the presence of God, angels, and this assembly, most solemnly and joyfully enter into covenant with one another, as one body in Christ.

We engage therefore, by the aid of the Holy Spirit, to walk together in Christian love; to strive for the advancement of this church, in knowledge, holiness, and comfort; to promote its prosperity and spirituality; to sustain its worship, ordinances, discipline, and doctrines; to contribute cheerfully and regularly to the support of the ministry, the expenses of the church, the relief of the poor, and the spread of the gospel through all nations.

We also engage to maintain family and secret devotion; to religiously educate our children; to seek the salvation of our kindred and acquaintances; to walk circumspectly in the world; to be just in our dealings, faithful in our engagements, and exemplary in our deportment; to avoid all tattling, backbiting, and excessive anger; to abstain from the sale and use of intoxicating drinks as a beverage, and to be zealous in our efforts to advance the kingdom of our Saviour.

We further engage to watch over one another in brotherly love; to remember each other in prayer; to aid each other in sickness and distress; to cultivate Christian sympathy in feeling and courtesy in speech; to be slow to take offence, but always ready for reconciliation, and mindful of the rules of our Saviour to secure it without delay.

We moreover engage that when we remove from this place, we will as soon as possible unite with some other church, where we can carry out the spirit of this covenant and the principles of God's word.

PRAYER

Now the God of Peace, who brought again from the dead our Lord Jesus, that Great Shepherd of the sheep, through the blood of the everlasting Covenant, make you perfect in every good work, to do his will; working in you that which is well-pleasing in his sight, through Jesus Christ; to whom be glory forever and ever. Amen.

CHAPTER IV

ORDINANCES OF A CHURCH

THIS title is not used to convey the idea that a church has the right to institute ordinances. No such right exists. The Lord Jesus Christ is head of the church—Lawgiver of the Gospel dispensation. He is the only Institutor of ordinances. Apostles had no discretion in the matter. They could only teach the baptized disciples " to observe all things " commanded by Christ. His will was to them, as to his followers, now the supreme law. It was optional with him to institute many ordinances or few. It was his pleasure to appoint only two, namely, Baptism and the Lord's Supper. These appointments of Christ are church ordinances in the sense that they pertain to his churches—not to the world; and are committeed to the care of his churches, whom he holds responsible for their preservation in their original purity and integrity. This does not mean that a congregation should feel free to make up its own rules about the ordinances. Instead, it should seriously ask how Christ wants them administered. It should look to the New Testament rather than to human traditions for guidance. Christ alone should control the ordinances, and each church is responsible to seek the mind of Christ in this, as in all matters.

Who recognizes the right of any man to preach or baptize, if unsustained by church authority? In this view of the matter baptism is evidently a church ordinance, and our Fathers in their Confession of 1689, refer to baptism and the Lord's Supper as Christ's ordinances " to be continued in his church to the end of the world."

I. OF BAPTISM

In answer to the oft-repeated question, What is Baptism? it may be said, Baptism is the immersion in water, by a proper administrator, of a believer in Christ, in the name of the Father, and of the Son, and of the Holy Spirit. Immersion is so exclusively the baptismal act, that without it there is no baptism; a believer in Christ is so exclusively the subject of baptism, that without such a subject there is no baptism. In these two statements all Baptists will agree. As to a proper administrator there may be some difference of opinion. By a proper administrator, in the foregoing definition, is meant a person who has received from a church authority to baptize. While the validity of an ordinance is not affected by every irregularity in its administration, it does seem incredible that baptism should be valid in the absence of the church authority referred to. What other authority is there? Will any one say, the authority of Christ? The supreme authority is undoubtedly his; but does he confer on men the right to baptize, *through his churches, or, independently of his churches?* One of these views must be taken, and he who takes the latter will have to set aside the order of the gospel. But it does not comport with the plan of this little work to elaborate this point.

1. ACT OF BAPTISM. That immersion alone is the baptismal act may be shown by the following considerations:

(1) *Greek Lexicons give immerse, dip, or plunge, as the primary and ordinary meaning of baptizo.*

Here it is proper to state that *baptizo* and *baptisma* are, in the Common Version of the

Scriptures, *Anglicized*, but not translated. By this it is only meant that their termination is made to correspond with the termination of English words. In *baptizo* the final letter is changed into *e*, and in *baptisma* the last letter is dropped altogether. To make this matter of Anglicism plain, it is only necessary to say, that if *rantizo* had been subjected to the same treatment by King James' translators which *baptizo* received at their hands, we would have *rantize* in the New Testament, wherever we now have *sprinkle*. King James virtually forbade the translation of *baptize* and *baptism*. This has sometimes been denied, but it is susceptible of conclusive proof. The king's third instruction to his translators reads thus: "The old *ecclesiastical words* to be kept, as the word *church* not to be translated *congregation*." It is absurd to say that this rule had exclusive reference to the term "" church "; for this term is manifestly given as a specimen of " old ecclesiastical words." And why should plurality of idea be conveyed by the phrase " ecclesiastical *words*," if the rule had respect to only *one word?* The question then is: Are *baptism* and *baptize* " old ecclesiastical words? They were *words* when the Bible was translated, or they would not be found in it. They had been used by church historians, and by writers on ecclesiastical law, and were therefore *ecclesiastical*. They had been in use a long time, and were consequently *old*. They were " old ecclesiastical words." Such words the king commanded " to be kept "—" not translated." It is worthy of remark too, that the Bishop of London, at the king's instance, wrote to the translators, reminding them that his majesty " wished his *third* and *fourth* rule to be specially observed." [1] This circumstance must have called special attention to the rule under consideration. In view of these facts it may surely be said, that the translators knew what were " old ecclesiastical words." Let their testimony then be adduced. In their " Preface to the Reader," they say they had " on the one side, avoided the scrupulosity of the Puritans, who left the *old ecclesiastical words,* and betook them to other, as when they put *washing* for *baptism,* and *congregation* for *church;* and on the other hand had shunned the obscurity of the Papists." Is not this enough? Here there is not only an admission that baptism was an old ecclesiastical

[1] Lewis' History of Translations, p. 319.

word, but this admission is made by the translators themselves—made most cheerfully—for it was made in condemnation of the Puritans, and in commendation of themselves.

The king's fourth rule was this: " When any word hath divers significations, *that* to be kept which hath been most commonly used by the most eminent Fathers, being agreeable to the propriety of the place and the analogy of faith." *Baptizo* is not a word of divers significations; but if it was, the king's translators, if they had rendered it at all, would have been compelled by the fourth rule to render it immerse; for every man of ordinary intelligence knows it was " most commonly used " in this sense " by the most eminent Fathers." But it will be perceived that the king's *third* rule renders inoperative the *fourth,* so far as old ecclesiastical words are concerned. Whether such words have one meaning or a thousand meanings, they are " to be kept "—" not translated." The translators were not at liberty to refer to the signification immemorially attached by the Greeks to *baptizo*—a signification which received the cordial indorsement of " the most eminent Fathers." They might have examined the indorsement if the royal

decree had not said, " *hitherto, but no farther,* "
" the old ecclesiastical words to be kept."

Some Baptist authors have expressed themselves as if King James had a special antipathy
to immersion, and forbade the translation of
baptizo and *baptism* with a view to encourage
sprinkling, which had been introduced from
Geneva into Scotland in the reign of Elizabeth,
and was in the early part of the seventeenth
century making its way into England. There
is no historical evidence that the king was opposed to immersion; but he was bitterly opposed to the " Genevan Version " of the Bible,
in which *baptism* was rendering *washing.*
Most probably his dislike of this version led
him to give his *third rule.* The Genevan Version was made by exiles from Scotland, who,
during the reign of " Bloody Mary," fled to
Geneva and became acquainted with John
Calvin.

The fact that *baptizo* is an *Anglicized,* and
not a translated word, makes an appeal to
Greek lexicons necessary in ascertaining its
meaning. Lexicons do not constitute the *ultimate* authority, but their testimony is valuable. There is a remarkable unanimity among
them in representing immerse or its equivalent

as the primary and ordinary meaning of the word. On this point Professor Stuart (long distinguished as the glory of the Andover Theological Seminary, Mass.) shall speak. In his treatise on the " Mode of Baptism," p. 14, he says, "*Bapto* and *baptizo* mean to · *dip, plunge,* or *immerge,* into anything liquid. All lexicographers and critics of any note are agreed in this." This quotation is made to supersede the necessity of giving the meaning of *baptizo* as furnished by the large number of Greek lexicons. Professor Stuart's statements will be received.

(2) *Distinguished Pedobaptist theologians. concede that baptizo means to immerse.*

John Calvin in his Institutes [1] says: " But whether the person who is baptized be wholly immersed, and whether thrice or once, or whether water be only poured or sprinkled upon him, is of no importance; churches ought to be left at liberty, in this respect, to act according to the difference of countries. The very word *baptize,* however, signifies to immerse; and it is certain that immersion was the practice of the ancient church."

Dr. George Campbell, a distinguished Pres-

[1] Vol. III, p. 491, edition of Presbyterian Board of Publication.

byterian of Scotland, in his "Notes" on Matthew 3 : 2, says: "The word *baptizein*" (infinitive mode, present tense, of *baptizo*) "both in sacred authors and in classical, signifies *to dip, to plunge, to immerse,* and was rendered by Tertullian, the oldest of the Latin Fathers, *tingere,* the term used for dyeing cloth, which was by immersion. It is always construed suitably to this meaning."

Doctor Chalmers, in his "Lectures on Romans" (Lecture XXX on Chap. VI, 3-7) says: "The original meaning of the word baptism is immersion, and though we regard it as a point of indifferency, whether the ordinance so named be performed in this way or by sprinkling—yet we doubt not that the prevalent style of the administration in the apostles' days was by an actual submerging of the whole body under water. We advert to this for the purpose of throwing light on the analogy that is instituted in these verses. Jesus Christ, by death, underwent this sort of baptism—even immersion under the surface of the ground, whence he soon emerged again by his resurrection. We, by being baptized into his death, are conceived to have made a similar translation."

This is a specimen of the concessions of learned Pedobaptists in regard to the meaning of *baptizo*. These concessions are of great value; for it may be said, in the language of another: " This testimony of theirs, to me, is worth a thousand others; seeing it comes from such as, in my opinion, *are evidently interested to speak quite otherwise.*"

(3) *The classical usage of baptizo establishes the position that immersion is the baptismal act.*

It has been already stated that lexicons are not the ultimate authority in settling the meaning of words. Lexicographers are dependent on the sense in which words are used, to ascertain their meaning. But it is not impossible for them to mistake that sense. If they do, there is an appeal from their definitions to the *usus loquendi,* which is the ultimate authority. It is well to go back to the ultimate authority. Want of room forbids the insertion of extracts from classical Greek authors; but it will be sufficient to refer to the treatise of Professor Stuart on the " Mode of Baptism." The reader will see that the learned professor in proving that *baptizo* means immerse, gives the word as used by Pindar, Heraclides Ponticus, Plutarch,

Lucian, Hippocrates, Strabo, Josephus, etc. Doctor Conant has investigated the meaning of *baptizo* more exhaustively than any man, living or dead. No use is made of his work, because Pedobaptist testimony is preferred. Seven hundred years intervened between the birth of Pindar and the death of Lucian. During those seven centuries usage shows that *baptizo* meant to immerse. Most of the classic Greek writers lived before baptism was instituted, and consequently knew nothing of immersion as a religious ordinance. Those who lived after its institution cared nothing for it. There was no controversy as to the meaning of *baptizo,* during the classic period of Grecian history. There was no motive, therefore, that could so operate on Greek writers as to induce them to use the word in any but its authorized meaning. That meaning was most obviously to immerse.

It is said by some that though *baptizo* in classic Greek means *immerse,* it has a different meaning in the New Testament. Let them prove it. On them is the burden of proof, and they will find it a burden they cannot manage. Let every man who takes this view answer this question: Could the New Testament writers, *as honest men,* use *baptizo* in a new sense without notifying their readers of the fact? It is certain they could not, and equally certain that no such notification was given.

(4) *The design of baptism furnishes a conclusive argument in favor of immersion.*

There is in baptism a representation of the burial and resurrection of Jesus Christ. Paul says: " Know ye not that so many of us as were baptized into Jesus Christ were baptized into his death? Therefore we were buried with him by baptism into death; that like as Christ was raised up from the dead by the glory of the Father, even so we should walk in newness of life. For if we have been planted together in the likeness of his death, we shall be also in the likeness of his resurrection " (Rom. 6 : 3-5). " Buried with him in baptism, wherein also ye are risen with him, through the faith of the operation of God who hath raised him from the dead " (Col. 2 : 12). Peter says: " The like figure whereunto even baptism doth also now save us (not the putting away of the filth of the flesh, but the answer of a good conscience toward God) by the resurrection of Jesus Christ " (1 Peter 3 : 21).

It is clear from these passages that baptism

has a commemorative reference to the burial
and resurrection of Christ. The two ordinances of the gospel symbolically proclaim the
three great facts of the gospel. These facts, as
Paul teaches (1 Cor. 15 : 3, 4), are that Christ
died, was buried, and rose again. The Lord's
Supper commemorates the first fact. At his
table the disciples of Christ are solemnly re-
minded that their Redeemer submitted to the
agonies of death. They weep over him as crucified—*dead*. In baptism they see him *buried*
and *raised again,* just as they see him *dead* in
the sacred Supper. Baptism is, therefore, a
symbolic proclamation of two of the three
prominent facts of the gospel—the burial and
resurrection of Christ.

Baptism also expresses, in emblem, the believer's death to sin, and resurrection to newness of life. In " repentance toward God and
faith toward our Lord Jesus Christ," there is a
spiritual death to sin, and a spiritual resurrection to newness of life. These two facts are
emblematically set forth in baptism. Hence
the absurdity of baptizing any who are not
dead to sin. We are baptized into the death
of Christ. We profess our reliance on his
death for salvation, and we profess, also, that

as he died *for* sin, we have died *to* sin. As burial is a palpable separation of the dead from the living, so baptism is a symbolic separation of those dead to sin from those living in sin. And as a resurrection from the dead indicates an entrance into a new sphere of existence, so baptism in its similitude to a resurrection denotes an entrance upon a new life. Hence Doctor Chalmers in the lecture already referred to says, that we " are conceived in the act of descending under the water of baptism, to have resigned an old life, and in the act of ascending, to emerge into a second or new life."

Baptism is likewise a symbol of purification. We read of the " washing of regeneration " and of having " our bodies washed with pure water." These forms of expression were most probably used to indicate the defiling nature of sin, from which we are really cleansed in the blood of Christ. Then baptism is the outward symbol of the inward washing. If any one should say the passages referred to will not bear this interpretation, be it so; but there is one passage that will bear it. " Arise and be baptized, and wash away thy sins, calling upon the name of the Lord," said Ananias to

Saul of Tarsus. " Wash away thy sins."
How? Literally? No, but symbolically. The
blood of Jesus really washes away sins. Hence
the language—" and washed us from our sins
in his own blood." But the sins which the
blood of Jesus has really washed away are
symbolically and formally washed away in
baptism.

Once more: Baptism anticipates the believer's resurrection from the dead. This we
learn from 1 Corinthians 15 : 29: " Else what
shall they do, who are baptized for the dead,
if the dead rise not at all? Why are they then
baptized for the dead? " These questions are
proposed in the midst of an argument on the
resurrection of the dead. Some of the Corinthians, it sems, denied the doctrine of the
resurrection, and yet it does not appear that
they questioned the propriety of an observance of the ordinance of baptism. Paul virtually tells them that baptism has an anticipa-
tive reference to the resurrection of the saints.
It has this reference, because it has a commemorative reference to the resurrection of
Christ. It anticipates because it commemorates.
The reason is obvious. The resurrection of
the Lord Jesus procures the resurrection of

his followers and is an infallible pledge of it. The two resurrections are inseparable. Baptism, therefore, while it commemorates the resurrection of Christ, anticipates, of necessity, the resurrection of his followers.

Now, if these views of the design and symbolic import of baptism are correct, it follows inevitably that the immersion, in water, of a believer in Christ, is essential to baptism—so essential that there can be no baptism without it. If baptism represents the burial and resurrection of Christ, it must be immersion. If it sets forth in emblem the believer's death to sin and resurrection to a new life, it must be immersion. If it in symbol washes away the sins which Christ has really washed away in his blood, still it must be immersion. And if it anticipates the resurrection, nothing but immersion justifies the anticipation. We are "buried by baptism"—that is, by means of baptism. When the baptismal process takes place there is certainly a "burial." The two are inseparable; and therefore, where there is no burial there is no baptism.

It had been our purpose to present a fifth consideration in favor of immersion, suggested by *the places selected for the administration of baptism, and the circumstances attending its administration, as referred to in the New Testament;* but the limits prescribed to this volume positively forbid.

2. SUBJECTS OF BAPTISM. While the import of the word baptize indicates what is the baptismal act, it does not determine *who* are to be baptized. We must, therefore, look elsewhere than to the meaning of the word to ascertain who are scriptural subjects of baptism. And where shall we look? To the commission given by Christ to his apostles; for this commission is the supreme authority for the administration of baptism. Apart from it there is no authority to baptize. The circumstances connected with the giving of this commisison were replete with interest. The Saviour had finished the work which he came down from heaven to accomplish. He had offered himself a sacrifice for sin. He had exhausted the cup of atoning sorrow. He had lain in the dark mansions of the grave. He had risen in triumph from the dead, and was about to ascend to the right hand of the Majesty on high. Invested with perfect mediatorial authority, he said to his apostles:

" All power is given to me in heaven and in

earth. Go ye therefore and teach all nations, baptizing them in the name of the Father, and of the Son, and of the Holy Ghost; teaching them to observe all things whatsoever I have commanded you" (Matt. 28 : 18-20). "Go ye into all the world and preach t1e gospel to every creature. He that believeth and is baptized shall be saved; but he that believeth not shall be damned" (Mark 16 : 15, 16). "Thus it is written, and thus it behooved Christ to suffer, and to rise from the dead the third day; and that repentance and remission of sins should be preached in his name among all nations, beginning at Jerusalem" (Luke 24 : 46, 47).

Surely the language of this commission is plain. Matthew informs us that teaching, or making disciples (for the verb *matheteuo* which he uses means *make disciples*) is to precede baptism; Mark establishes the priority of faith to baptism; and Luke connects repentance and remission of sins with the execution of the commission. No man can, in obedience to this commission, baptize an unbeliever or an unconscious infant. The unbeliever is not a penitent disciple, and it is obviously impossible for the infant to repent and believe the gospel.

It may be laid down as a principle of common sense, which commends itself to every candid mind, that *a commission to do a thing authorizes only the doing of the thing specified.* The doing of all other things is virtually forbidden. There is a maxim of law, that *the expression of one thing is the exclusion of another.*[1] It must necessarily be so; for otherwise there could be no definiteness in contracts, and no precision in legislative enactments or judicial decrees. This maxim may be illustrated in a thousand ways. Numerous scriptural illustrations are at hand. For example: God commanded Noah to make an ark of *gopher-wood.* He assigns no reason why gopher-wood should be used. The command, however, is positive, and it forbids the use of every other kind of wood. Abraham was commanded to offer his son Isaac for a burnt-offering. He was virtually forbidden to offer any other member of his family. Aye, more, he could not offer an animal till the order was revoked by Him who gave it, and a second order was given, requiring the sacrifice of a ram in the place of Isaac. The institution of the Passover furnishes an illustration, or rather

[1] Expressio unius est exclusio alterius.

a combination of illustrations: A lamb was to be killed—not a heifer; it was to be of the first year—not of the second or third; a male—not a female; without a blemish—not with a blemish; on the fourteenth day of the month—not on some other day; the blood was to be applied to the door-posts and lintels— not elsewhere.

The Constitution of the United States supplies many illustrations, only two of which will be mentioned. It provides that " the President shall have power, by and with the advice and consent of the Senate, to make treaties, provided two-thirds of the senators present concur." Does any sane man believe the Supreme Court and the House of Representatives can make treaties? Or that the President without the Senate, or the Senate without the President, can make treaties? The Constitution in giving the treaty-making power to the President and Senate virtually forbids all others to make treaties.

Again, the Constitution says: " The President, Vice-president, and all civil officers of the United States, shall be removed from office on impeachment for and conviction of treason, bribery, or other high crimes and misdemeanors." Here one method of removal from office is prescribed, and all other methods are prohibited. Every man understands this.

In application of the principle laid down and of the law maxim illustrated, it may be affirmed, that the commission of Christ, in enjoining the baptism of disciples, believers, prohibits, in effect, the baptism of all others. It will not do to say, we are not forbidden, in so many words, to baptize infants. The same may be said of unbelievers; aye, of horses, cattle, and bells.

It will be said by those who oppose the views of Baptists—for it has been said a thousand times—that if infants are not to be baptized because they cannot believe, they will not be saved, because they cannot believe. If the salvation of infants depends on their faith, they cannot be saved. They are incapable of faith. They are doubtless saved through the mediation of Christ, but it is not by faith. Our opponents fail egregiously to accomplish their object in urging this objection to our views. They must intend to make us admit the propriety of infant baptism, or force us to a denial of infant salvation. But we make neither the admission nor the denial. As soon as we say that infants are saved, not by faith, but without faith, their objection is demolished.

In considering the commission of Christ it is well to observe how it was understood and carried into effect in apostolic times. The first practical interpretation of it was given on the day of Pentecost. The gospel was preached, the people were pierced to the heart, and cried out, " Men and brethren, what shall we do? " Peter replied, " Repent, and be baptized every one of you." No man will say that the command " Repent," is applicable to infants, and it is certain the same persons were called on to *repent and be baptized*. The result of Peter's sermon is seen in the following words: " Then they that gladly received his word were baptized: and the same day there were added to them about three thousand souls." The baptism was limited to those who gladly received Peter's words; and as infants were not of that number, to infer that they were baptized is utterly gratuitous. The Pentecostal administration of baptism shows that penitent believers were considered the only subjects of the ordinance.

Philip's labors in Samaria indicate his understanding of the Great Commission. He preached Christ to the people. What then? The people "believed Philip preaching the things concerning the kingdom of God and the name of Jesus Christ." What next? "They were baptized, both men and women." Here again baptism was restricted to believers.

Was this rule deviated from among the Gentiles? Certainly not. When Peter preached to Cornelius and his dependents, there was a restriction of baptism to those who received the Holy Spirit; and when Paul preached in Corinth "many of the Corinthians hearing, believed, and were baptized."

Thus it appears that among Gentiles, as well as Samaritans and Jews, baptism was preceded by faith in Christ. Thus does it appear that the commission was practically expounded in the same way both in Europe and Asia.

Nor do the household baptisms mentioned in the New Testament furnish any argument against the baptism of believers alone; for something is said of every household which could not be said of unconscious infants. For example, it is said of Cornelius (Acts 2 : 2), that he " feared God *with all his house;* of the jailer (Acts 16 : 32, 34) that Paul and Silas " spake to him the word of the Lord, and *to all that were in his house,"* and that he " rejoiced, believing in God *with all his house."* It is said of Lydia (Acts 16 : 40) that Paul and Silas having been released from prison, entered into her house, " and when they had seen the brethren, they comforted them." Doubtless " *the brethren"* were persons in Lydia's employ who constituted her " household," and were baptized as well as herself. Infants would not have been called *brethren,* nor referred to as *comforted.* The intimation in Acts 18 : 8 is that the family of Crispus was baptized, but it is said he " believed on the Lord *with all his house."* Paul, as we learn from 1 Corinthians 1 : 16, baptized the household of Stephanas, but he says in the same epistle (16 : 15): " Ye know the house of Stephanas, that it is the first fruits of Achaia, and that they have addicted themselves to the ministry of the saints." These are all the household baptisms mentioned in the New Testament, and we see in them no deviation from the commission of Christ, which requires *discipleship* as prerequisite to baptism. On the other hand, they confirm the position, that believers alone are scriptural subjects of baptism.

The allusions to baptism in the apostolic epistles forbid the supposition that infants were baptized. Paul refers to the " baptized " as " dead to sin "—rising from the baptismal waters to " walk in newness of life "—as " putting on Christ "—as " baptized for the dead," or in the belief of the resurrection. Peter defines baptism to be " the answer of a good conscience toward God." This is a general definition which precludes the idea that baptism was, in apostolic times, administered to any except accountable agents. What conscience has a speechless infant? There is no operation of conscience prior to accountability. Baptism, then, in its administration to infants, cannot be what Peter says it is.

Without enlarging on these topics, what is the conclusion of the whole matter? Clearly this: The commission of Christ, as understood and exemplified in the apostolic age, requires the baptism of believers, disciples; and the baptism of all others, whether adult unbelievers or unconscious infants, is utterly unwarranted. There is, as Paul has said, ONE

BAPTISM. It is *one* in the action involved, and *one* in the subject of the action.

II. THE LORD'S SUPPER

What Paul says of the institution and design of the Lord's Supper is the substance of what the evangelists had recorded. These are his words: " For I have received of the Lord that which also I delivered to you. That the Lord Jesus the same night in which he was betrayed took bread: and when he had given thanks, he brake it, and said, Take, eat: this is my body, which is broken for you: this do in remembrance of me. After the same manner also he took the cup, when he had supped, saying, This is the new testament in my blood: this do ye, as oft as ye drink it, in remembrance of me. For as often as ye eat this bread and drink this cup, ye do show the Lord's death till he come " (1 Cor. 11 : 23-26).

From this inspired account of the origin of the Lord's Supper it is plainly a commemorative institution. It commemorates chiefly and supremely the death of Christ. " Ye do show the Lord's *death*." We do not show the birth, or baptism, or burial, or resurrection, or ascension of our Redeemer, *but his death.* If ever the tragedy of Calvary should engross the thoughts of the Christian to the exclusion of every other topic, it is when he sits at the table of the Lord. Then the death of his Lord should monopolize all the power of memory.

> Remember thee! thy death, thy shame!
>   The griefs which thou didst bear!
> O memory, leave no other name
>   But his recorded there.

Some will perhaps say, that in the Lord's Supper we express our Christian fellowship for our fellow communicants. This is done only in an indirect and incidental manner. Our communion, according to Paul, is the communion of the body and blood of Christ. It is a solemn celebration of his atoning death.

Baptists, with comparatively few exceptions, have ever considered baptism a prerequisite to the Lord's table. They have so regarded it, because they have recognized its indispensableness to church-membership. They have reasoned in this way: The Lord's Supper is an ordinance to be observed exclusively by the members of a visible church of Christ. As the

Lord's Supper is a church ordinance it is not proper to administer it to persons in their individual capacity—for example, to the sick at their homes. The meeting of a *church* is indispensable to a scriptural observance of the solemn feast. None can be members of a visible church of Christ without baptism. Therefore, baptism is a prerequisite to communion at the Lord's table. It will be seen from this statement of the case, that baptism is a prerequisite to the Lord's Supper because it is a prerequisite to church-membership. Church-membership is the chief condition anterior to communion at the Lord's table. Baptism is a condition precedent only in the sense that it precedes, and is essential to church-membership. It would be well for Baptists to make this view more prominent. Let them not say less of baptism, but more of church-membership. In Acts 11 : 41 it is said: " Then they that gladly received his word were baptized, and the same day there were added to them about three thousand souls." The three thousand were no doubt added to the church, " the hundred and twenty disciples," mentioned in the preceding chapter; for in the last verse of the second chapter it is written: " And the

Lord added to the church daily such as should be saved." The adding in the two verses was the same in kind—that is, it was an adding to the church. It will be perceived that the *baptized* were added to the church, and that this was done before the " breaking of bread "— a phrase descriptive of the Lord's Supper. A refusal on the part of Baptists to commune with Pedobaptists grows out of the fact that the latter have ever been considered by the former as unbaptized, and consequently with · out a scriptural church-membership.

Even the celebrated Robert Hall, who advocated the intercommunion of Baptist and Pedobaptists, with an eloquence and energy of argumentation rarely to be found in the annals of controversy, does not hesitate to express the opinion that Pedobaptists are unbaptized. He says:

" We certainly make no scruple of informing a Pedobaptist candidate that we consider him as unbaptized, and disdain all concealment upon the subject." Again, " If we join with those whom we are obliged to consider as unbaptized, they unite with persons who, in their judgment, repeat an ordinance which ought not to be performed but once, nullify a Christian institute and deprive their children of the benefit of a salutary rite." [1]

But while Mr. Hall considered Pedobaptists unbaptized, he insisted on their right as *unbaptized* persons to come to the Lord's table. He did not admit baptism to be a prerequisite to communion. Had he conceded this, a point almost universally conceded by Baptists and Pedobaptists, he would not have written his " Terms of Communion " at all.

To demolish all that Robert Hall ever wrote in favor of " Mixed Communion," it is only necessary to show the scriptural priority of baptism to the Lord's Supper. And surely this is not difficult to do. That baptism was first instituted, is a significant fact. No one will deny that John, the harbinger of Christ, baptized multitudes, and that Jesus through his disciples (John 4 : 1, 2) baptized more than John, before the institution of the Lord's Supper. It is morally certain that those present at its institution, the night of the betrayal, had been baptized. Jesus himself had been baptized, and it is too much for credulity itself to believe that he selected unbaptized persons as his apostles. Does the subsequence of the

[1] Hall's Works, Vol. I, pp. 455, 456.

Lord's Supper, in its original appointment, to baptism, mean nothing? But it was said by Mr. Hall, that " John's baptism was not Christian." It was gospel baptism. It was not an ordinance of the Mosaic economy. John certainly introduced the gospel dispensation. His preaching was " the beginning of the gospel " (Mark 1 : 1) and " the law and the prophets were until John " (Luke 16 : 16). If any one chooses to deny that his baptism was *Christian* because it is not so termed, the denial may be so enlarged as to embrace all the baptisms of the New Testament; for the epithet Christian is not applied to any of them.

But while firmly believing that John's was a gospel ministry and a gospel baptism, all this might be waived by Baptists, for argument's sake, and then they can show the unavoidable priority of baptism to communion. Let them go at once to Christ's last commission: " Go, teach all nations, baptizing them." Every scholar knows the Greek term translated " teach " means *disciple*, or *make disciples*. Disciples to Christ were to be made through the preaching and teaching of the apostles. This is plain. The discipling process was first, and then the baptismal act was to be performed. " Go, disciple all nations, baptizing them." Now, according to the commission, it is evident that the process of discipleship is to be so immediately followed by the administration of baptism, as to leave no room for an observance of the Lord's Supper to intervene. Baptism is the first thing after a person is discipled to Christ. It is the believer's first public duty. It is the first external manifestation of his internal piety. It is an open avowal of allegiance to Christ. It is, therefore, inevitably prior to the Lord's Supper, an observance of which is no doubt included in the expression: " Teaching them to observe all things whatsoever I have commanded you." The baptized disciples are to be taught to observe all things which he has commanded. Under the commission of Christ his ministers are not required to say anything about the Lord's Supper to the unbaptized. The baptized disciples are to be instructed. How then can the Lord's Supper precede baptism, when the commission enjoins the mention of it only to the baptized?

But how did the apostles understand and carry into effect this commission? This is a question of capital importance in this discus sion. On the day of Pentecost, Peter said to the convicted Jews, " Repent, and be baptized." The baptism was to succeed the repentance. There is no intimation that the Lord's Supper was to come between. And it is added, that the baptized " continued steadfastly in the apostles' doctrine and fellowship, and in breaking of bread, and in prayers." The breaking of bread—the Lord's Supper— was preceded by baptism. When Philip went down to Samaria and preached, the people believed, and " were baptized, both men and women." The narrative plainly indicates that baptism, and not the Lord's Supper, immediately followed the people's belief of what Philip preached. When the Ethiopian eunuch avowed his faith in Christ, Philip at once baptized him. There was no celebration of the Lord's Supper before they left the chariot and " went down into the water." When Cornelius and his house received the Holy Spirit, Peter did not ask who can forbid the Lord's table to them, but, " Can any man forbid water, that these should not be baptized?" When Paul and Silas, at the hour of midnight, preached to the jailer and his family, and they believed what was then done? Did they commune at the Lord's table? No, but he and all his were baptized immediately.

Thus does it appear that the apostles and primitive ministers understood the commission as enjoining baptism before the Lord's Supper. They have left an instructive example, which we are not at liberty to disregard. In view of this example we may boldly affirm, that the whole tenor of the New Testament indicates the priority of baptism to communion. Nothing is plainer.

Pedobaptists concede the precedence of baptism to the Lord's Supper. Doctor Wall, in his "History of Infant Baptism," Part II, Chap. IX, expresses himself in strong terms as follows:

"No church ever gave the communion to any persons before they were baptized. Among all the absurdities that ever were held, none ever maintained that any persons should partake of the communion before they were baptized."

Doctor Doddridge, in his "Miscellaneous Works," p. 510, remarks:

"It is certain that Christians in general have always been spoken of, by the most ancient Fathers, as baptized persons. And it is also certain that, as far as our knowledge of primitive antiquity extends, no unbaptized person received the Lord's Supper."

Doctor Hibbard, a Methodist author of considerable distinction, in his work on " Christian Baptism," thus expresses himself:

" It is but just to remark, that in one principle the Baptist and the Pedobaptist churches agree. They both agree in rejecting from communion at the table of the Lord, and in denying the rights of church fellowship to all who have not been baptized. Valid baptism they consider as essential to constitute visible church-membership. This, also, we hold. The only question then that here divides us is, what is essential to valid baptism? The Baptists, in passing a sweeping sentence of disfranchisement upon all other Christian churches, have only acted upon a principle held in common with all other churches, viz.: that baptism is essential to church-membership. . . Of course, they must be their own judges as to what baptism is. It is evident that, according to our views, we can admit them to our communion; but with their views of baptism, it is equally evident, they can never reciprocate the courtesy; and the charge of *close communion* is no more applicable to the Baptists than to us; inasmuch as the question of church-membership is determined by as liberal principles as it is with any other Protestant churches—so far, I mean, as the present subject is concerned, *i. e.,* it is determined by valid baptism." (Hibbard's " Christian Baptism," pp. 171, 175.)

This extract from Doctor Hibbard exhibits a spirit of controversial candor and fairness, not often witnessed in the discussion of the communion question. It explodes the charge of " Baptist bigotry and exclusiveness," and establishes the fact that the point in dispute between Baptists and others is not about *close communion,* but *close baptism.* The controversy is supremely and intensely baptismal.

Every visible church of Christ may be considered a sacred inclosure, susceptible of entrance in but one way. In that inclosure is set the table of the Lord. And the Lord of the table has prescribed the terms of admittance into that inclosure. Those who have complied with the terms and have entered in, are the guardians of the table. They must see to it that it is approached only in the way which the Lord of the inclosure and of the table has specified. If they are appealed to, to change the entrance way, or to make a new entrance, or to allow those without to make ways of entrance to suit themselves, they must say with strongest emphasis: "THERE IS ONE LAWGIVER"—"WE HAVE NO SUCH CUSTOM, NEITHER THE CHURCHES OF GOD."

It will be said—for it has been said, no one knows how often—the table is the Lord's. This all will concede. But how different are the reasonings based on this concession! Pedobaptists say, as it is the Lord's table they have a right to approach it—that as it is not the table of the Baptists, the Baptists ought not to place obstructions in the way of their approach. Baptists say, as it is the Lord's table, it must be approached in the way he directs—that his proprietorship of the table furnishes the reason of their course—that if it was their table they would have discretionary authority, whereas they now have none—that *they* do not place obstructions in the way of Pedobaptists, but that the Lord of the table has done it. This is a specimen of the logic employed by the two parties in the controversy. Which species of logic indicates greater loyalty to Christ, the reader may determine.

CHAPTER V

THE GOVERNMENT OF A CHURCH

THERE are three forms of church government, indicated by the terms Episcopacy, Presbyterianism, and Congregationalism.

Episcopacy recognizes the right of bishops to preside over districts of country, and one of its fundamental doctrines is, that a bishop is officially superior to other ministers. Of course, a modern bishop has under his charge the " inferior clergy "; for it is insisted, that the " ordaining power," and " the right to rule," belong to the Episcopal office. Those who adopt the Episcopal form of government believe that there are three orders in the ministry—namely, deacons, elders, and bishops. The modern application of the term bishop to a man who has under his charge a district of country, is very objectionable. It has almost banished from Christendom the idea originally attached to the term. In apostolic times, bishop, pastor, and elder were terms of equivalent import. The elders of the church of Ephesus are termed (Acts 20 : 24) *overseers*—in the original, *episcopos*—the word generally translated "bishop," if indeed "bishop" may be called a translation.

Presbyterianism recognizes two classes of elders—*preaching* elders and *ruling* elders. The pastor and ruling elders of a congregation constitute what is called the "session of the church." The "session" transacts the business of the church, receives, dismisses, excludes members, etc. From the decisions of a session there is an appeal to the presbytery; from the action of the presbytery an appeal to the Synod; and from the action of the Synod an appeal to the General Assembly, whose adjudications are final and irresistible.

Congregationalism antagonizes with Episcopacy and Presbyterianism, and distinctly recognizes these truths:

1. *That the governmental power is in the hands of the people.*

It resides with the people in contradistinction from bishops or elders—that is to say, bishops or elders can do nothing, strictly and properly ecclesiastic, without the concurrence of the people.

2. *The right of a majority of the members of a church to rule, in accordance with the law of Christ.*

The will of the majority having been expressed, it becomes the minority to submit.

3. *That the power of a church cannot be transferred or alienated, and that church action is final.*

The power of a church cannot be delegated. There may be messengers of a church, but there cannot be delegates in the ordinary sense of the term. It would be well for the churches in their letters to associations and councils, to say *messengers,* not *delegates.* No church can empower any man, or body of men, to do anything which will impair its independency.

These are highly important principles, and while the existence of the congregational form of church government depends on their recognition and application, it is an inquiry of vital moment: Does the New Testament inculcate these principles? For if it does not, whatever may be said in commendation of them, they possess no obligatory force.

Does the New Testament then inculcate the foundation principle of Congregationalism;

namely, *that the governmental power· of a church is with the members?* Let us see.

It was the province of the apostolic churches to admit members into their communion.

In Romans 14 : 1 it is written: "Him that is weak in the faith receive ye." The import of this language obviously is, "Receive into your fellowship and treat as a Christian him who is weak in faith." There is unquestionably a command—RECEIVE YE. To whom is this command addressed? To bishops? It is not. To the " Session of the church," composed of the pastor and the ruling elders? No. To whom then? To the very persons to whom the epistle was addressed, and it was written " to all that be in Rome, beloved of God, called to be saints." No ingenuity can torture this language into a command given to the officers of the church in Rome. The members of the church, whose designation was " saints," were addressed and commanded to " receive the weak in faith." It was their business to decide who should be admitted into their Christian community; and Paul under the impulses of inspiration, says, " Him that is weak in the faith, receive ye."

We now proceed to show that the New Testament churches had the right to exclude unworthy members, and that they exercised the right.

In 1 Corinthians 5 : 1-5 we read as follows: "It is reported commonly that there is fornication among you, and such fornication as is not so much as named among the Gentiles, that one should have his father's wife. And ye are puffed up, and have not rather mourned that he that hath done this deed might be taken away from among you. For I verily, as absent in body, but present in spirit, have judged already, as though I were present, concerning him that hath so done this deed; in the name of our Lord Jesus Christ, when ye are gathered together, and my spirit, with the power of our Lord Jesus Christ, to deliver such an one to Satan, for the destruction of the flesh, that the spirit may be saved in the day of the Lord Jesus."

It is worthy of remark that while Paul "judged" that the incestuous man ought to be excluded from the church, *he* did not exclude him. He did not claim the right to do so; and when he said to the "churches of Galatia," "I would they were even cut off who trouble you," he did not cut them off, though he desired that it should be done.

It deserves notice too, that the members of the Corinthian church could not, in their *individual capacity*, exclude the incestuous man. It was necessary that they should be " gathered together." They must assemble as a church. Thus assembling. " the power of our Lord Jesus Christ " was to be with them. They were to act by his authority, and execute his will; for he makes it incumbent on his churches to exercise discipline. In the last verse of the chapter referred to, Paul says: " Put away from among yourselves that wicked person." Here is a command, given by an inspired man, requiring the exclusion of an unworthy member from the church at Corinth. To whom was the command addressed? To the official members of the church? No; but " to the *church* of God, which is at Corinth, to them that are sanctified in Christ Jesus, called to be saints."

The right of a church to exclude from its communion disorderly persons is recognized in 2 Thessalonians 3 : 6: " Now we command you, brethren, in the name of our Lord Jesus Christ, that ye withdraw yourselves from every brother that walketh disorderly." This command was addressed " to the *church* of the Thessalonians." To withdraw from a " disorderly brother " is the same thing as to exclude him. There is a cessation of church fellowship.

Matthew 18 : 17 has not been referred to, because it will be noticed in another place. The reader will see, upon examination, that the passage clearly implies the power of " the church " to perform the act of excommunication, by which the member cut off becomes " as a heathen man and a publican."

The apostolic churches had the power and the right to restore excluded members who gave satisfactory evidence of penitence.

In 2 Corinthians 2 : 6-8 the " incestuous man is again mentioned, as follows: " Sufficient to such a man is this punishment, which was inflicted of many. So that contrariwise ye ought rather to forgive him and comfort him, lest perhaps such an one should be swallowed up with overmuch sorrow. Wherefore I beseech you that ye would confirm your love toward him." The apostle manages this case with the greatest tenderness and delicacy. He refers to the excluded member without the least reference to the disgraceful offence for which he was excluded. " Sufficient," says he, " is this punishment," etc. That is, the object of the exclusion had been accomplished. The church had shown its determination not to connive at sin, and the excluded member had become penitent. But the point under consideration is, that the apostle advised the restoration of the penitent offender. Paul could no more restore him to the church than he could expel him from it in the first instance; but he says, " I beseech you that ye confirm your love toward him." The power to restore was with the church, and Paul solicits an exercise of that power. The great apostle in saying, *" I beseech you,"* bows to the majesty of democratic church sovereignty. He virtually admits that nothing could be done unless the church chose to act.

Now, if the New Testament churches had the power and the right to receive, exclude, and restore members, they must have had the right to transact any other business coming before them. There surely can be nothing more vital to the interests of a church than the reception, exclusion, and restoration of members. Here we might let the argument for the foundation principle of congregationalism rest; but there is other proof of the recognition of that principle.

In the first chapter of the Acts of the Apostles there is an account of the election of Matthias to the apostleship. He was to succeed Judas, the traitor. The most natural inference is, that Matthias was chosen by the " one hundred and twenty disciples " mentioned in verse 15. These disciples were, no doubt, the church to which the three thousand converts were added on the day of Pentecost. The people must have been held in high estimation by Peter, if called on in conjunction with the apostles themselves to elect a successor to Judas.

In Acts 6 there is reference to the circumstances which originated the deacon's office, and also to the manner in which the first deacons were appointed. It will be seen that the matter of grievance was referred by the apostles to the *multitude of the disciples*— that they directed the *brethren to look out seven men*—that the saying pleased *the whole multitude*—and *they chose, etc.* The words we have *italicized* render the agency of the people in the whole transaction clear as the sun in heaven. Not only the *disciples,* but the *multitude,* the *whole multitude* of the disciples acted. No language could more strongly express the action of a church, as distinguished from that of its officers.

In support of the fundamental principle of Congregationalism, the following facts are stated: The " whole church "—the " brethren "—are named in connection with the " apostles and elders " Acts 15 : 22, 23 : " Then pleased it the apostles and elders, *with the whole church,* to send chosen men. . . And they wrote letters by them after this manner: ' The apostles, and elders, and *brethren,* send greeting.' " The brethren of the church at Jerusalem acted, as well as the apostles and elders.

The churches of apostolic times sent forth ministers on missionary tours. When Antioch received the word of God, the church at Jerusalem " sent forth Barnabas, that he should go as far as Antioch " (Acts 11 : 22). His labors were successful—" much people was added to the Lord "—and at a subsequent period the church in Antioch sent out Saul and Barnabas, who made a long journey, performed much labor, returned, and reported to the *church* all that God had done with them. (Acts 13 : 1-3; 14 : 26, 27.) With what deferential respect did these ministers of the gospel treat the church that sent them forth! The apostles, so far from exercising lordship over the churches, did not control their charities. This is seen in Acts 11 : 29, 30; 1 Corinthians 16 : 1, 2; 2 Corinthians 9 : 7. The churches selected messengers to convey their charities. (See 1 Cor. 16 : 3; 2 Cor. 8 : 18, 19; Phil. 2 : 25; 4 : 18.)

A second principle of Congregationalism, already announced, is *the right of a majority of the members of a church to rule in accordance with the law of Christ.*

In 2 Corinthians 2 : 6 it is written, " Sufficient to such a man is this punishment, which was inflicted of many." A literal translation of the words rendered " of many," would be " by the more "—that is, by the majority. McKnight's translation is, " by the greater number." If, as has been shown, the governmental power of a church is with the members, it follows that a majority must rule. This is so plain a principle of Congregationalism, and of common sense, that it is needless to dwell upon it.

A third truth, recognized by the Congregational form of church government is, *that the power of a church cannot be transferred or alienated, and that church action is final.*

The church at Corinth could not transfer her power to the church at Philippi, nor could the church at Antioch convey her authority to the church of Ephesus. Neither could all the apostolic churches combined delegate their power to an association, or synod, or convention. That church power is inalienable results from the foundation principle of Congregationalism—that this power is in the hands of the people, the membership. And if the power of a church cannot be transferred, church action is final. That there is no tribunal higher than a church is evident from Matthew 18 : 15-17. The Saviour lays down a rule for the adjustment of private differences among brethren. "If thy brother shall trespass against thee go tell him his fault," etc. If the offender, when told of his fault, does not give satisfaction, the offended party is to take with him, one or two more, that in the mouth of two or three witnesses every word may be established." But if the offender "shall neglect to hear them," what is to be done? "Tell it to the church." What church? Evidently the particular congregation to which the parties belong. If the offender does not hear the church, what then? "Let him be unto thee as a heathen man and a publican." But can there be no appeal to an association, or presbytery, or conference? No. There is no appeal. Shall an association, or presbytery, or conference put the offender back in church fellowship, when the church, by its action, classed him with heathens and publicans? This is too preposterous. What kind of fellowship would it be? Will it be asked, what is to be done if the action of a church does not give satisfaction to all concerned? What is to be done when the action of a Presbyterian General Assembly, or Methodist General Conference, or an Episcopal General Convention does not give satisfaction? There must be a stopping-place. There must be final action. Baptists says, with the New Testament before them, that the action of each local congregation of believers is final. Pedobaptists, with the exception of Independents and Congregationalists, deny the *finality* of church action.

Who are right? Let those who oppose the Baptist form of church government show in the New Testament the remotest allusion to an appeal from the decision of a church to any other tribunal. It cannot be done.

The view here presented of the independence of the apostolic churches is so obviously in accordance with the facts of the case that distinguished Pedobaptists have been forced to concede it. Hence Mosheim, a Lutheran, and a bitter enemy of Baptists, speaking of the first century, says: "The churches in those early times were entirely independent, none of them being subject to any foreign jurisdiction, but each governed by its own rulers and its own laws; for, though the churches founded by the apostles had this particular deference shown to them, that they were consulted in difficult and doubtful cases, yet they had no juridical authority, no sort of supremacy over the others nor the least right to enact laws for them." [1]

Archbishop Whately, a dignitary of the Church of England, referring to the apostolic churches, says: "They were each a distinct, independent community *on earth,* united by

[1] Maclaine's "Mosheim's Church History," Baltimore edition, Vol. I, p. 39.

the common principles on which they were founded, and by their mutual agreement, affection and respect; but not having any one recognized Head on earth, or acknowledging any sovereignty of one of these societies over others." Again: "A CHURCH and a DIOCESE seem to have been for a considerable time *coextensive* and *identical*. And each church or diocese, though connected with the rest by ties of faith, and hope, and charity, seems to have been perfectly independent as far as regards any power of control." [1]

This is strong testimony from a Lutheran and an Episcopalian. They would have given a different representation of the matter, if they could have done so consistently with truth. They virtually condemned their own denominational organizations in writing thus.

Before closing this chapter, it may be proper to say that while a church in the exercise of its independence may receive members excluded from another church, it cannot be done, *in ordinary circumstances,* without a violation of church courtesy, and a departure from the spirit of the gospel. It is assumed that, as a general thing, members are *deservedly* ex-

---

[1] "Kingdom of Christ," Carter's edition, pp. 36, 44.

cluded from church fellowship. When this is
the case, it is manifestly improper for them to
be received by sister churches. It would have
been a flagrant violation of propriety for any
other church to have received to its membership the incestuous man expelled by the church
at Corinth. Those justly excluded, if they
would enjoy church privileges again, must
penitently confess the offenses for which they
were excluded, and obtain restoration to membership in the church from whose fellowship
they were cut off. This is the general rule.
Sometimes, however, a member is unjustly excluded. Prejudice or party feeling may control the action of the church. In the exercise
of discipline the law of Christ may be departed
from. Acknowledgments which ought to be
satisfactory may be declared insufficient. The
arraigned member is unjustly expelled. The
impression, it may be, is made on the community, as well as on sister churches, that the expulsion is unjust. What is to be done? The
excluded member is suffering wrongfully, and
earnestly desires to enjoy church privileges.
The church that has passed the excluding act
ought to rescind it. Suppose, however, the
church, disregarding the advice of disinter-

ested, judicious brethren, does not rescind its act. Then the expelled member, the injustice of his exclusion being known, may be rightfully received into the fellowship of another church Such cases rarely occur; but when they do, it is well to know that they may be disposed of in the manner here suggested. There is in church independence ample authority for this course of procedure. THE ACTS OF A CHURCH ARE VALID AND BINDING WHEN THEY ACCORD WITH THE LAW OF CHRIST: WHEN THEY DO NOT THEY ARE NULL AND VOID.

CHAPTER VI

THE DISCIPLINE OF A CHURCH

IF discipline is necessary in families, schools, and armies, it must answer important purposes in the churches of Christ. It may be considered the process by which the spiritual improvement, usefulness, and efficiency of a church are promoted. In its comprehensive sense church discipline is both *formative* and *corrective,* though the phrase is generally used in the latter acceptation. We notice briefly.

I. FORMATIVE DISCIPLINE

The doctrine of formative discipline is taught in such passages as these: " In whom all the building fitly framed together groweth unto a holy temple in the Lord: in whom ye also are builded together for a habitation of God through the Spirit." " For the perfecting of the saints, for the work of the ministry, for the edifying of the body of Christ; till we all come in the unity of the faith, and of the knowledge of the Son of God, unto a perfect man, unto the measure of the stature of the fullness of Christ." " Giving all diligence, add to your faith virtue; and to virtue knowledge; and to knowledge temperance; and to temperance patience; and to patience godliness; and to godliness brotherly kindness; and to brotherly kindness charity." " Grow in grace, and in the knowledge of our Lord Jesus Christ " (Eph. 2 : 21, 22; 4 : 12, 13; 2 Peter 1 : 5-7; 3 : 18).

It is clear from these Scriptures that Christians should ever be in a state of progressive spiritual improvement. They must not retrograde, nor remain stationary, but be constantly advancing in the divine life. The " perfecting of the saints " is an object of vast importance. The perfection referred to has to do, not so much with absolute freedom from sin, as some suppose, as with the symmetrical development and maturity of Christian character. The new convert to the faith of the gospel is a " babe," a spiritual infant, that has " need of milk," and not of " strong meat." Formative church discipline contemplates the vigorous growth of the " babe in Christ " till it is developed into " a perfect man." Bringing the baptized disciples into local church organizations has this purpose in view. They are to be taught " to observe all things whatsoever Christ has commanded." By such observance alone can a church edify itself in love, building up its members on their most holy faith. By such observance is promoted the symmetry of Christian character, and in it are included all the activities of the Christian life.

Formative discipline, in its sanctifying influences, ought to reach every church-member. The old, with their gray hairs, should exhibit its beneficial power in the ripeness of the fruits of the Spirit. The middle-aged, in the perfection of physical strength, should also show that it makes them " strong in the Lord and in the power of his might." And the young, in the morning of life, should yield to its plastic touches, that they may become useful laborers in the vineyard of the Lord. All have been redeemed with the precious blood of Christ and " should live, not to themselves, but to him who died and rose again."

If every church will experimentally and practically learn the lessons taught in 1 Corinthians 12 : 12-27, the subject of formative discipline will be well understood. Then no member will be dissatisfied with his own place, and envy the place of another. No one will attach undue importance to his own services, and undervalue the services of others. No one will forget that the "more feeble members" of a church are "necessary," because they have something to do. There will be cordial sympathy and cooperation growing out of identity of spiritual interests. Such a church will prosper and "grow unto a holy temple in the Lord." But if a church fails to learn the lessons referred to, its members will make comparatively no progress in the divine life—they will remain in a state of spiritual infancy—and their knowledge of the gospel will be so meager and superficial as to subject them to the charge brought against the Hebrews: "For when for the time ye ought to be teachers, ye have need that one teach you again which be the first principles of the oracles of God; and are become such as have need of milk, and not of strong meat. For every one that useth milk is unskillful in the word of righteousness: for he is a babe" (Heb. 5: 12, 13).

II. CORRECTIVE DISCIPLINE

This phrase implies the imperfection of church-members—their liability to sin. Alas.

how many are the proofs of this imperfection—how numerous the illustrations of this liability! Jesus said, "It must needs be that offences come." Depravity makes this certain in society at large; and the remains of depravity render it certain in individual Christians and in Christian churches. In every case of church discipline the honor of Christ and the interests of his cause are more or less affected; and it deserves special notice that the Saviour's injunctions contemplate disciplinary church action as the last resort. Everything else that can be done must first be done to adjust differences and remove offences among brethren. There are two commands of Christ, which, if, faithfully obeyed, would in almost every instance prevent personal offences from assuming such form and magnitude as to require church action. These injunctions are to be found in Matthew 5 : 23, 24 and 18 : 15, and they are as follows: *"Therefore if thou bring thy gift to the altar, and there rememberest that thy brother hath ought against thee: leave there thy gift before the altar, and go thy way; first be reconciled to thy brother, and then come and offer thy gift."* *"Moreover, if thy brother trespass against thee, go and tell him his fault between thee and him alone."*

According to the former of these passages the brother who is supposed to be the offender is to go to the offended brother. He must go promptly. The necessity of an immediate interview between the parties is so imperative as to justify the suspension of an act of worship till the interview is held. "Leave there thy gift before the altar." The form of expression was no doubt suggested by the sacrificial arrangements of the Mosaic economy. The person addressed is supposed, after getting to the altar, to remember that his brother has something against him. He must not say: "My brother ought not to have anything against me—I have done him no injury—he is laboring under a false impression—his grievance is not real, but imaginary—and it is needless to go to him," etc. But the Master says, "Leave thy gift at the altar, and go." Dare the servant disobey his Lord? Let him go and show the offended brother that he has no just cause of complaint, that he is under a false impression, if this is the case. But if, at the altar of God, he remembers that he has done his brother injustice, let him go, if possible, more promptly and, confessing his fault, seek reconciliation. The observance of this first injunction of Christ would lead to the adjustment of a thousand differences among brethren. But, according to the second command, there is something for the offended party to do. "If thy brother trespass against thee, go and tell him his fault between thee and him alone." The offended brother is not to wait till the offender goes to him and seeks reconciliation. The offender may not know that he has given offence—that "his brother has aught against him." Or if he knows it, he may neglect his duty. This, however, does not affect the obligations of the offended brother. There must be an interview between the parties. The offender, as we have seen, is required to go to the offended, and the offended is required to go to the offender; and should they both start at once and meet midway it would be so much the better. It would show such a spirit of obedience to Christ as would make the settlement of the difficulty morally certain. "Tell him his fault between him and thee alone." The offended brother is, at this stage of the proceeding, to tell the offender his fault. He must let no one know what he is going to do.

He must not ask the advice of any one. He
needs no advice. Nothing can be plainer than
the command of Christ. " Tell him his fault."
This is to be done orally.[1] A word is used in
the original which suggests the idea of presenting reasons or proofs to convince of a
fault. The offended brother is to do this, and
if he does, the offender is to acknowledge his
fault, ask forgiveness, and there the matter is
at an end. If, however, the proofs presented
are shown by the accused brother to be insufficient to establish the charge against him,
let the party making the charge cheerfully re-
tract it, with expressions of gratification that
it is not true, and with expressions of regret
that it had been made. Neither party should
ever mention the subject again.

TWO CLASSES OF OFFENCES

It has been common to refer to offences requiring discipline as *private* and *public*. These

---

[1] It has sometimes occurred that the offended brother has
chosen to write to the offender rather than state his grievance
by word of mouth. This is very reprehensible. Christ does
not say " write a note or a letter," but " go and tell him his
fault." In ninety-nine cases out of a hundred the inclination
to write would indicate a wrong spirit. It would betray an
unchristian desire to get some advantage, especially if the
offended one believed he could wield the pen more effectively
than the offender. The language of the Master is, " Tell him
his fault."

epithets of designation are, perhaps, not the best that could be selected. By a *private* is meant a *personal* offence, but a personal offence may be publicly committed. Hence the word *private* is inadequate to express the full idea intended to be conveyed. A *public* offence as distinguished from a private one is an offence committed in public; but as distinguished from a *personal* offence it is committed against a church in its collective capacity. It may be committed too, in secret, or in comparative secrecy. For example, theft, with whatever privacy perpetrated, is against good morals, and is therefore what is usually called a public offence. We prefer the use of the epithets *personal* and *general* to designate offences. They are sufficiently descriptive for all practical purposes. There might be a third class of offences termed *mixed*—that is partly personal and partly general—but we confine this discussion to the two classes indicated.

1. *Personal.* What is a personal offence? It is an offence against an individual. " If thy brother shall trespass against *thee*." Any offence committed by one brother against another, which, if acknowledged and forgiven by the parties, would leave the fellowship of the

church undisturbed, is personal. Such an offence, whether committed in private or public, has to do with the two brethren, and not with the church. It cannot be brought before the church legitimately till the directions of Christ, in Matthew 18 : 15, 16, are complied with. The offended brother, presuming to bring his grievance before the church, in disregard of these directions, would subject himself to church censure; and the church by considering the grievance would violate the law of her Head. The more this law is studied the more will its wisdom be seen; and the less surprise will be felt at the unhappy consequences resulting from its neglect.

In all personal offences the rule to be observed is plain: " If thy brother shall trespass against thee, go and tell him his fault between thee and him alone: if he shall hear thee thou hast gained thy brother." The object of the offended brother must be to *gain* the offender. If this is not his purpose, he violates the *spirit* of Christ's law though he may obey it in the *letter*. He must earnestly hope and pray, that he may be so successful in this first step as not to find it necessary to take the second. It is sometimes the case—it is humiliating to admit it—that the first step is taken in an unbrotherly spirit, with the hope that the second will have to be taken, and then the third, so that the offender will be, as speedily as possible, put in the place of " a heathen man and a publican." When this is so it is not hazarding much to say that the offended brother is as censurable as the offender.

" If he hear thee, thou hast gained thy brother." It is easy to see that the Saviour refers to this as the accomplishment of an important object which should gratify the aggrieved brother's heart. " Thou hast gained thy brother." What an acquisition, and how sublime the satisfaction arising therefrom! And it may be said, the offending brother is generally gained when there is a sincere desire to gain him expressed, in earnest prayer, that he may be gained. If the brother is gained, proceedings happily end, and the dearest friends of the parties must not know, if the offence is a private one, that the adjusted difficulty ever existed. Or if the personal offence has been publicly committed it is enough for it to be known that the matter has been satisfactorily settled. It is better not to talk about the details of the adjustment.

But there will be cases in which the offending brother is not "gained." What then is to be done? The second step to be taken is this: "If he will not hear thee, then take with thee one or two more, that in the mouth of two or three witnesses every word may be established." The brethren selected by the aggrieved brother to go with him should be very judicious and eminently spiritual. Sound judgment and ardent piety will be needed. If the charge made by the plaintiff in the case is denied by the defendant—that is, if there be an issue of veracity between the parties—and no third person knows anything of the matter, it must be dropped. The "one or two more" present must so advise and insist. The parties concerned stand on a perfect equality as members of the church, and the veracity of the one is to be considered as unquestionable as that of the other. It will not do for the brethren whom the offended brother has taken with him to yield a credence to his statements which they withhold from the statements of the other. Whatever may be their *private* opinions as to the Christian and moral character of the parties, they must be treated alike. Hence we repeat, that if there is an issue of veracity, on which no third person can shed light, the case must be dropped.

But the Saviour's language supposes that the case may be continued. The offender may not deny the charge brought against him, but may attempt to justify himself as to the thing complained of. It may be evident to the " one or two more " who are present, that he has a wrong spirit, and that, from his own account of the matter he has given the aggrieved brother just cause of offence. Here then is the place for them to exercise Christian judgment and show the spirit of the gospel. They must, if possible, convince the offender of his fault, and secure from him a reparation of the injury he has done the offended brother. If he is convinced that he has done wrong, and makes a satisfactory acknowledgment, it must be received. Or, if the acknowledgment is not satisfactory to the aggrieved brother, while those he has taken with him think it should be, they must say so, and urge him to accept it. It must be the object of their anxious desire to have the difference adjusted in accordance with the law of Christ. If this is done, let the parties concerned say nothing more about the matter, and let the brethren who have aided in the adjustment hold their peace.

But there is another supposition: It is supposed that a reconciliation may not be effected and that the " one or two more " may be called to testify as witnesses before the church. " That in the mouth of two or three witnesses every word may be established." Now the third and last step is to be taken by the offended brother: " Tell it to the church." The church, till this point is reached, has nothing to do with the matter. The discipline, strictly speaking, has not been church discipline, but the discipline of brethren in their individual character. In a meeting of the church the aggrieved brother states that, in his judgment, he has just cause of offence against a fellow member, and asks permission to present the facts in the case. The pastor, or presiding officer, must inquire of him if he has gone to the offending brother and told him his fault, no third person being present? If he answers in the negative, the pastor must tell him kindly, but firmly, that he cannot be permitted to state his grievance. If he answers in the affirmative, the pastor must ask him if he with " one or two more " has gone to the offending

brother, taking the second step enjoined by
Christ. If he answers negatively, the pastor
must say: "The rule which governs us will
not permit you to tell your grievance to the
church till the second step is taken as well
as the first." If he answers affirmatively, he
can name the brethren he took with him,
who can corroborate his statement. The pastor can then say, according to the law of
Christ, you can now make your statement.
He tells his grievance to the church. The
offender, it may be, admits that the cause of
complaint is stated just as it was at the two
previous interviews, or if he says it is not, the
witnesses can testify as to the statement made
in their presence. Every word said at the
second interview between the parties is to be
established by the witnesses. The offender
may still attempt to justify himself. The witnesses may repeat the arguments they used to
convince him that he was in the wrong; and
the church seeing him in the wrong, may admonish him to make reparation of the injury
he has done. If the offender should, at this
point in the proceedings, "hear the church"—
that is, carry her advice into practical effect—
the matter ends and he retains his member-

ship. But, " If he neglect to hear the church, let him be unto thee as a heathen man and a publican." The intimation here is, that a refusal to hear the church will be followed by the act of exclusion, which is a public withdrawal of fellowship. Having been excluded he becomes to the offended member, and to all the members, " as a heathen man and a publican." There is a cessation of Christian intercourse.

2. *General Offences.* It has been stated that a general offence, as distinguished from a personal one, is committed against a church in its collective capacity. That is to say, it is committed against no member in particular, but against all the members in general—against one member as much as another. To this definition it may be added that while all general offences are against churches as bodies, some are, and some are not, violations of the law of public morals. For example, drunkenness, theft, lying, etc., violate the law of morality, and may be considered offences against society at large as well as against the churches of Christ; but the espousal of false and heretical doctrines by a church-member, though an offence against the church, is not a crime against

society. It does not invade the domain of public morals.

While it does not comport with the limits or the design of this volume to give an exhaustive catalogue of general offences, it is believed that the most of them may be classified as follows:

1. *A rejection of any of the fundamental doctrines of the gospel.* According to the constitution of the human mind the denial of fundamental truth is the belief of fundamental error. The apostle Paul attached great importance to what he termed " the truth of the gospel," and knowing that he had preached the gospel in its purity to the Galatians, he said: " Though we, or an angel from heaven, preach any other gospel unto you than that which we have preached unto you, let him be accursed. As we said before, so say I now again. If any man preach any other gospel unto you than that ye have received, let him be accursed " (Gal. 1 : 8, 9). The beloved disciple, proverbial for kindness of heart, said with great firmness, " If there come any unto you, and bring not this doctrine, receive him not into your house, neither bid him God speed. For he that biddeth him God speed is

partaker of his evil deeds " (2 John 10, 11). As the gospel is the charter of the church's incorporation, it is plain that a denial of any of the essential doctrines of the gospel is an offence against the church, and calls for its disciplinary action. And then too, every church by virtue of its constitution is the guardian of " the truth as it is in Jesus." How can its guardianship be effective, if it does not put fundamental errorists without the pale of its fellowship? Paul said to Titus: " A man that is a heretic. after the first and second admonition, reject." The term " heretic " in this passage, no doubt, means an instigator of divisions; but why does the heretic become such an instigator? Because, ordinarily, he has embraced false doctrines which place him in antagonism with the church, and make him the head of a faction. He is, therefore, a proper subject of church discipline. It will be observed that reference has been made to fundamental errors, and these errors are supposed to be inconsistent with true piety. There are errors, however, of a lower grade, which, while they do not promote piety, are not subversive of it. With regard to these a judicious toleration must be exercised—such a toleration as is suggested by the words of the apostle: "Him that is weak in the faith receive ye." While in the flesh, individual Christians and Christian churches will find it necessary to bear with errors in sentiment and imperfections in practice; but they must tolerate nothing which is virtually subversive of the gospel. Loyalty to Christ forbids this.

2. *Anything that seriously disturbs the union and peace of a church.* The New Testament teaches nothing more plainly than, that while a church meets together " in one place," it should be " of one accord, of one mind." Its members are required to be united in love; for while truth is the basis, love is the cement of their union. How reasonable that they love one another, and that out of their love should grow a union sacred and inviolable! They are children of the same Father—redeemed by the same blood—regenerated by the same Spirit—baptized into the same body—bound by solemn covenant to live according to the gospel—and animated with the bright prospect of immortal glory. Surely there should be union and peace among the members of such a congregation of the Lord.

Alas, the union may be disturbed—the peace broken. The seeds of discord may be sown and everything thrown out of harmony. This was sometimes the case in the days of the apostles. Hence Paul says: " Mark them which cause divisions, and offences, contrary to the doctrine which ye have learned; and avoid them. For they that are such serve not our Lord Jesus Christ." The union and peace of a church may not only be disturbed by the espousal of false doctrines, but also by the adoption of false views of church polity. Suppose a member, for instance, while holding to what are termed " the doctrines of grace," should deny the necessity of regeneration in order to church-membership, or the necessity of immersion in order to baptism, or should have his own children christened in infancy, or should insist on the right of unbelievers to come to the table of the Lord; every one can see that the union and peace of a church, organized according to the scriptural model, would be seriously disturbed. Such a disturber would deserve church discipline, and fidelity on the part of his offended brethren would institute the process without delay.

3. *Disorderly and immoral conduct in all
its forms*. There is reference to disorderly
conduct in the following passages: " Now we
command you, brethren, in the name of our
Lord Jesus Christ, that you withdraw yourselves from every brother that walketh disorderly. . . For we hear that there are some
which walk among you disorderly, working
not at all, but are busybodies " (2 Thess. 3 :
6, 11). For a church to withdraw from a disorderly brother is equivalent to his exclusion.
There is a cessation of church fellowship.

In the subjoined passage *immoral* conduct
is referred to. " But now I have written unto
you not to keep company, if any man that is
called a brother be a fornicator, or covetous,
or an idolater, or a railer, or a drunkard, or
an extortioner; with such an one no not to
eat " (1 Cor. 5 : 11). These terms, so expres-
sive of immorality, are used, no doubt, to denote specimen classes of wicked persons. The
term fornicator, for example, is to be understood as embracing all those who commit
sexual iniquities. There is no express mention
of murderers, liars, thieves, etc., but they are
unquestionably included, with all other wicked
characters, as guilty of general offences which

call for church action. Alas, that these offences so often occur.

How general offences are to be treated. The impression prevails, to a great extent, that, because general offences are committed against a church as a body, they need not be treated after the manner of personal offences. True, they cannot be treated alike in all respects, but there should not be such a difference of treatment as is often seen. In some churches there is scarcely a private, personal effort made to convince of their guilt those who have committed general offences. This is wrong. A *heretic* is guilty of a general offence; but, according to Paul, he is not to be rejected till " after the first and second admonition." The reference is no doubt to the program of discipline as arranged by Christ in Matthew 18. It cannot be too earnestly urged that private, personal effort be made with brethren who have committed *general* offences. They will be much more likely to show a Christian spirit when thus dealt with than when their offences are, without preliminary steps, made the subject of church investigation. These private, personal exertions are considered proofs of kindness, and there is something in human nature which revolts and rebels against public exposure. In Galatians 6 : 1, 2 it is written: " Brethren, if a man be overtaken in a fault, ye which are spiritual restore such an one in the spirit of meekness, considering thyself, lest thou also be tempted. Bear ye one another's burdens, and so fulfill the law of Christ." It will be seen that the restoration of the offender is the object to be sought. It is to be sought by the " spiritual " in the " spirit of meekness." While prosecuting this object they are to consider their own liability to be overcome by temptation, and make necessary allowances for the offending brother. They are, as nearly as possible, to place themselves in his position, and take on their hearts the burden which, it may be, is crushing his. This would be fulfilling the law of Christ—that law is love; and love prompts us to bear the burdens of those we love. When the inspired directions of the apostle are faithfully followed, the brother " overtaken in a fault " usually confesses it, and gives satisfaction to those seeking his restoration. This is an auspicious result, and it must be announced at the next meeting of the church. The offence having been general, the church must be satisfied. Ordinarily, what satisfies the brother or brethren seeking the offender's restoration satisfies the church.

Sometimes the most earnest exertions to reclaim a brother fail of success. Then the case must be brought before the church. The facts connected with it must be stated. The arraigned member must have ample opportunity to defend himself. If his defence is satisfactory to the church the matter goes no farther. Or if the brother, while the investigation is going on, becomes convinced of his guilt and makes confession, the church must forgive him. If, however, the offence is established by conclusive proof, and there is no penitence leading to confession, the act of exclusion must take place. The church must withdraw its fellowship.

Offences of an infamous or scandalous character must have a peculiar treatment. The church must express its reprobation of them by an immediate act of exclusion. No preliminary steps are necessary. No penitence must prevent the withdrawal of fellowship. The honor of Christ and the purity of his religion are especially involved in these cases. What Paul says in regard to the incestuous man (1 Cor. 5) vindicates the position here taken. If a church-member is guilty of adultery, or murder, or perjury, or theft, or forgery, or drunkenness, or any kindred crime, he deserves exclusion without trial. Some perhaps would except drunkenness from this catalogue, but taking into account the manifold evils of intemperance, in connection with the light shed on the "temperance question" for thirty years past, one instance of drunkenness makes it the duty of a church promptly to exercise its power of excommunication. No church can adequately express a suitable abhorrence of such offences without excluding the offender. Nor can the world be otherwise convinced that the church is the friend and the conservator of good morals.

HOW EXCLUDED MEMBERS OUGHT TO BE TREATED

This is a question of no little importance; for the practical answer to it has much to do with the effect of church discipline. Social intercourse with the excluded is not to be entirely suspended; for then many opportunities of doing them good will be lost: neither is it to be just as before the exclusion; for that would impair the efficacy of discipline. The members of a church must so act toward those they have expelled as to give the expulsion its legitimate moral influence. The apostle Paul lays down this rule: " If any man that is called a brother be a fornicator, or covetous, or an idolater, or a railer, or a drunkard, or an extortioner; with such an one no, not to eat " (1 Cor. 5 : 11). That is, we must not keep company with such an one. There must be no such social familiarity as the excluded may construe into a connivance at their offences. Andrew Fuller well remarks: " If individual members act contrary to this rule, and carry it freely toward an offender, as if nothing had taken place, it will render the censure of the church of none effect. Those persons also who behave in this manner will be considered by the party as his friends, and others who stand aloof as his enemies, or at least as being unreasonably severe; which will work confusion, and render void the best and most wholesome discipline. We must act in concert, or we may as well do nothing. Members who violate this rule are partakers of other men's sins, and deserve the rebukes of the church for counteracting its measures." [1] We dismiss the topic by a reference to 2 Thessalonians 3 : 14, 15: " And if any one obey not our word by this epistle, note that man, and have no company with him that he may be ashamed. Yet count him not as an enemy, but admonish him as a brother."

OBJECTS TO BE HAD IN VIEW IN DISCIPLINE

Prominent among these objects are:

1. *The glory of God.* Whatever makes corrective church discipline necessary dishonors God. The greater its necessity the more is God dishonored. The need of discipline in all its stages arises from the fact that there is a state of things in conflict with the will of God. Whatever is in conflict with his will tarnishes his glory. If then God is to be honored, and his glory promoted in the churches, discipline must be exercised to correct that which is in conflict with his will, and which obscures his glory. Our God is infinitely holy, and the neglect of discipline, when either personal or general offences require it, virtually represents him as the patron of

[1] Works, Vol. III, pp. 334, 335.

iniquity. Let the churches tremble at this thought, and remember that the holy God they serve is also a jealous God.

2. *Purity of the Churches.* The followers of Christ, though in the world, are not of the world. They are called out of darkness into marvelous light—called to be saints—called with a holy calling—and in their embodied form as churches they are the depositaries of the pure principles of the gospel. They are Christ's representatives in the world—lights of the world, cities set on hills which cannot be hidden. Paul said to the Corinthians: " Be ye not unequally yoked together with unbelievers: for what fellowship hath righteousness with unrighteousness? and what communion hath light with darkness? And what concord hath Christ with Belial? or what part hath he that believeth with an infidel?" (2 Cor. 6 : 14, 15). These significant questions show that the spirit of Christianity and the spirit of the world are utterly irreconcilable. And if so, the churches of the saints, to maintain their purity, must apply the rod of corrective discipline to all who live unworthily of the gospel. They must do this to vindicate " the truth as it is in Jesus," and to represent his

religion as the antagonist of whatever is evil. With special reference to the necessity of expelling an unworthy member (1 Cor. 5 : 1) an apostle says, " Know ye not that a little leaven leaveneth the whole lump?" As if he had said, "Are you ignorant that the retention of a flagrant transgressor will corrupt the entire church?" The purity of the churches cannot be preserved without faithful discipline. And every church virtually endorses the wrongs she does not, by disciplinary action, attempt to correct.

3. *The spiritual good of the disciplined.* This is a third object to be kept in view in all disciplinary proceedings. We have seen already that in matters of personal offence the " gaining " of the offending brother is to be specially regarded. Those who have been " overtaken in a fault " are, if possible, to be restored. And when a church passes an act of exclusion—delivering a member over to Satan—that is, *formally* transferring him from Christ's jurisdiction to that of the devil—it must be done, " *that the spirit may be saved in the day of the Lord Jesus.*" There must be no bitterness of feeling, no disposition to persecute and oppress, no indulgence of revenge-

ful impulses. The act of expulsion must be considered a *painful* necessity, and should be passed by the church with great solemnity and pronounced by the pastor with a still greater solemnity. Everything should be so done as to make the impression on all that it is an awful thing to be cut off from the fellowship of God's people. It would be well for an earnest prayer to be offered that the disciplinary action may prove a blessing to the offender, exert a salutary influence on the church, and impress the community with the *holiness* of the religion of Jesus.

It is suggested that it might be well for every pastor, the next Lord's Day after the exclusion of a member, to announce the fact to the congregation. Sometimes a church is considered by men of the world as endorsing an unworthy character because they do not know of the act of exclusion. It should, in some way, be made known.

CHAPTER VII

DUTIES OF A CHURCH

THOUGH some of the duties of a church have been incidentally referred to in preceding chapters, the subject is too important to be dismissed without a more distinct consideration. It is plain that Christ, in providing for the formation of churches, recognized and sanctified the social principle. A church is a society—a social institution. Its members, while they sustain a supremely sacred relation to their Head, sustain important relations to one another. They are "no more strangers and foreigners, but fellow citizens with the saints and of the household of God" (Eph. 2 : 19). In this passage two metaphors are employed, one of which represents a church as a commonwealth, and the other as a family. Fellow citizens with the saints, of a spiritual commonwealth, is one of the apostle's conceptions. This citizenship denotes a state the opposite of that indicated by the term " strangers and foreigners," or rather strangers and *sojourners*. The citizen has duties to perform and privileges to enjoy, which do not concern the stranger at all, and the sojourner to a very limited extent. The citizen occupies not only an honorable, but a responsible position, and fellow citizens are expected to act in concert. The other conception of the apostle represents a church as a household, a family of God. A literal translation would be *domestics of God*—that is, belonging to his family. The point we make is that the members of a church, whether considered as fellow citizens of God's commonwealth, or as belonging to his family, have something to do. Their duties are urgent, imperative, sacred.

1. *They owe duties to one another*. Paul in one place refers to the self-edification of a church. His language is " unto the edifying of itself in love." There is something at fault with every church that does not build itself up on its most holy faith. There should be constant growth in grace. And as the thrifty plant or vigorous tree grows in all its parts, so should there be spiritual growth in all the members of a church. They must abound in

supreme love to Christ and in fervent love for one another.

Christian love is the great duty of church-members, which, when faithfully performed, secures the performance of all other duties that they owe one another. If they remember the words of Jesus—" a new commandment give I unto you that ye love one another "— they will not forget the many ways in which this love may express itself. Toward the pastor it will show itself in respect for his teachings, in obedience to his admonitions, and in imitation of his example, so far as he follows Christ. It will provide an adequate pecuniary support for him that he may give himself to his work, unperplexed with cares concerning the things of this life.

Christian love will prompt the members of a church to do good to one another as they have opportunity. " To do good " is a very comprehensive phrase. It is generic and includes under it all the specific methods of doing good. It embraces all forms of labor for the welfare of the body and specially those which concern the soul. It does not overlook the interests of time, but looks supremely to the interests of eternity.

There is another inspired expression deserving special notice—"forbearing one another in love." This implies that church-members will have occasion to exercise their forbearance. Alas, they often have. Their long-suffering is tried, their patience put to the test. Sometimes it seems wonderful how much they can bear and forbear. It would be inexplicable, but for the words, " IN LOVE " forbearing one another in love. Love covers a multitude of faults. It makes Christians look leniently on the frailties, weaknesses, and imperfections of their fellow Christians. It makes them bear patiently what they cannot approve, and bear it till it assumes a form that calls for the exercise of that discipline which the Lord Jesus has given his churches " for edification, and not for destruction." " Forbearing one another in love " would be a suitable church motto.

In treating of the duties which church-members owe one to another, it is well to refer briefly to the duty of

Seeking out and encouraging whatever ministerial gifts there may be in the membership. This is a very important matter. We doubt not there are many young men in our churches who ought to preach the gospel. They have impressions on the subject. They look on the work of the ministry as so responsible that they recoil from it with trembling. They feel their incompetency; and, in view of ministerial duties and trials, repeat the stereotyped question, " Who is sufficient for these things? " These are the very men who need to be sought out and encouraged. Their views of the greatness of the work of preaching the gospel are correct. Their self-distrust is altogether commendable. The ablest of the Lord's ministers once felt as they now feel. They need instruction. Let them be encouraged to speak and exhort in prayer-meetings, and soon it will be seen that they possess ministerial gifts. It devolves specially on pastors, and the more judicious of the brethren, to train these *future* ministers for usefulness; and, wherever money is needed for the education of any of them, the churches ought cheerfully to furnish it. There is no pecuniary investment so productive as that made in ministerial education. But it must ever be remembered that piety is the preacher's first and most important qualification, without which the greatest talents, and the richest stores of learning, will make him as "sounding brass or a tinkling cymbal."

2. *A church owes duties to the world.* The term world is here used to denote impenitent sinners. Every Christian by the very process which makes him a Christian is brought under obligation to do what he can to lead others to Christ. And when individual believers are embodied in churches their obligations not only remain in full force, but the facilities of usefulness are increased. Church-members must recognize these obligations, and avail themselves of these facilities. They must labor for the salvation of souls under the distinct impression that the grace which has saved them can save others. Thus only can they labor in faith and hope. The following are some of the methods in which church-members may perform their duties to impenitent sinners.

1. *By personal conversation with them about their souls.* Christians must not forget that the faculty of speech has been given for important purposes, and should be used accordingly. Few things are more to be desired among church-members than a consecration of the power of speech. Conversational talent

needs to be improved and sanctified. How can the tongue be so worthily employed as in speaking of the "great salvation"? What theme so momentous, so precious, so sublime? Christians must not only "speak often one to another," but they must converse with the impenitent about their souls.

It is not important that their ideas be presented with logical precision and rhetorical beauty; but it is indispensable that the love of Christ animate their hearts and prompt their speech. The members of every church should see to it that every impenitent sinner within the bounds of the congregation is conversed with on the subject of religion and urged to accept the salvation of the gospel. It must not be said in truth by even one of the unregenerate "no man cared for my soul." Such a declaration truthfully made would be a reproach to any church. Let it not be made; but let church-members show their interest in the welfare of the impenitent by personal conversation with them on the weighty concerns of eternity.

2. *By the maintenance of Sunday Schools.* The Sunday School is not designed to supersede, but to aid family instruction. It must

be remembered always that religious training in the family cannot be dispensed with. Parental obligations can no more be transferred than parental relations can be changed. But it may be assumed as a fact, that those parents who are most faithful in " bringing up their children in the nurture and admonition of the Lord," most gladly avail themselves of the aid furnished by Sunday School instruction. And then how many ungodly parents are to be found everywhere who are incompetent to give their children religious training, and who would not, if they were competent! Are these children to be uncared for? No, nor those whose parents are dead. The sympathies of all generous hearts are enlisted in behalf of orphans. All children are suitable subjects for the Sunday School. Whether their parents are pious, or ungodly, or dead, let all the children be gathered together to receive religious training on the Lord's Day. Superintendents and teachers of Sunday Schools must remember that scriptural instruction is the one thing to be kept in view. Literary instruction, properly so-called, is given in week-day schools. The impartation and reception of scriptural knowledge are the distinguishing features of the Sunday School. Great care should be exercised in the selection of books for church libraries. Books with erroneous views must be rejected, and the literature provided for the children must be religious and evangelical.

Sunday School teachers should make it a point to urge, by personal appeal, the claims of the gospel on every scholar. Every such appeal ought to be preceded, accompanied, and followed by earnest prayer to God for his blessing. Without his favor no effort to do good will be successful; with his approving smile no effort will be unsuccessful.

It is proper to say a few words as to the relation of Sunday Schools to the churches. Ordinarily, these schools are formed by the churches and are permitted to use their houses of worship. They should be carried on under the general direction of the churches, and be held responsible thereto. A church should regard its Sunday School as one of the agencies by which to meet its obligations to train the rising generation in the fear of God. And when this is the case the church is really at work in the Sunday School. It would be a happy circumstance if facts would authorize this definition of a Sunday School: A CHURCH ACTIVELY AT WORK ON THE LORD'S DAY FOR THE GOOD OF THE CHILDREN.

" The classes in the school," it has been well said, " should be composed, not simply of *children,* but also of the grown-up people in the neighborhood—grandfathers and grandmothers, fathers and mothers, and men and women. The school should be considered one of the regular meetings of the church. Pastors should summon the *entire* people to assemble on the Lord's Day, either as teachers or as scholars. It should be considered as strange for fathers and mothers to stay away from the Bible classes as for boys and girls to absent themselves from the Sunday School. That pastor who will speak to his congregation on this topic three minutes before sermon each Lord's Day for one year, and then work to get up classes as he may be able through the week, will be astonished at the results. And ten years of such efforts by all the ministers of the gospel would work a complete revolution in the churches. Instances might be given to show that a church sometimes more than doubles its power by employing its private members in this way."

3. *By the distribution of the Bible, religious books, tracts, etc.* This is another method by which a church may do good to the impenitent. God has given to the world one book. It is unlike all other books. It carries with it, wherever it goes, the credentials of its inspiration and claims the reverence due to a communication from heaven. The Bible is God's gift to the world. It was not given to the white man, nor the red man, nor the black man, *as such,* but to universal man. This volume alone unfolds the way of salvation by telling the wonders of the cross. It is revealed truth by means of which the soul is regenerated, sanctified, and prepared for heaven. Who is to see to it that this precious book is distributed at home and abroad? It cannot be reasonably expected that God's enemies will do it. His friends must engage in the work. They know something of the value of the Bible, and their sense of its worth must prompt them to circulate it. Every church should consider itself, by virtue of its constitution, a Bible Society, and should aid in the great work of disseminating divine truth throughout the world. It is a question that may well be pondered with solemn interest: *Will God,*

in his providence, long permit any people to retain his word, if that people do not give it to others? Let every church think of this.

The distribution of religious books, tracts, and periodicals is a work kindred to the circulation of the Scriptures. Religious books are reproductions and expositions of some of the truths of the inspired volume. A good book brings a portion of divine truth into contact with the conscience and heart. And this is the reason why the unobtrusive tract is so useful.

A special use should be made of the tracts and pamphlets that set forth the distinctive principles of the denomination. The various Baptist conventions have their publishing agencies, which supply a variety of materials. Copies of these should be circulated by hundreds of thousands. As a people, we claim that certain great truths have been committed to our care. For what did the Lord commit them to us?—to pass them over as unimportant? We dare not do this. These principles are not ours to do with as may seem most agreeable. They are Christ's. He has honored us with their custody, not for ourselves, but for others. Upon us he has placed the especial responsibility of commending them. In common with all other Christians it is our duty to bear testimony to all truths, but *specially to our distinctive principles.* We owe it to ourselves, we owe it to Christ our Lord, and we owe it to our brethren dearly beloved, but in error, to make known these principles to the very utmost of our ability.

The mission of Baptists will not be attained by apologizing to the world for an existence, by asking pardon of other denominations for differing from them, or by begging that we may not be esteemed as bigots. We must become aggressive in spirit, positive in the advocacy of our principles.

And these truths can be made known best by the free and wide-spread circulation of our denominational tracts, pamphlets, and books. Let them, then, be widely used. Information about materials should be secured from the appropriate denominational publisher. What a great, far-reaching power might be called into being by the churches, if they would but address themselves with determination and perseverance to the gradual but perpetual distribution of these tracts, pamphlets, and books!

How greatly might converts be guarded from erroneous views and practices, be indoctrinated in the principles of the gospel and faith of the church, and be made substantial Christians, if with the hand of fellowship, the pastor could give to each one received the best small work on Baptism, another on Communion, and another still on the Duties of Church-members! And the pastor should not hesitate to ask the church to supply him with these aids in his work.

4. *By sustaining the cause of missions.* The missionary enterprise is usually referred to in its two aspects—home and foreign. There is full scriptural authority for the presentation of both these aspects. The commission of Christ to the apostles of itself furnishes it: "Go ye into all the world, and preach the gospel to every creature: He that believeth and is baptized shall be saved; but he that believeth not shall be damned" (Mark 16 : 15, 16). It is clear from this commission that the gospel is to be preached at home and abroad; for it is to be preached in all the world. It is to be proclaimed to all the nations; for it is to be proclaimed to every creature. "Ye shall be witnesses unto me

both in Jerusalem, and in all Judea, and in Samaria, and unto the uttermost part of the earth" (Acts 1 : 8). This was the program of missionary labor in apostolic times. How suggestive the words, *Jerusalem—all Judea— Samaria—uttermost part of the earth.* This was the plan and zealously was it executed.

It may be laid down as an axiom that no church, not animated with the missionary spirit, can be in a healthful, prosperous state. The missionary spirit is the spirit of the gospel—the spirit of Christ. Of every church it ought to be said in truth as of the Thessalonians : " From you sounded out the word of the Lord." The sound should go forth till it reaches the remotest limits of the earth. It is the sound of the word of the Lord. The word of the Lord is the gospel by which sinners of all nations may be saved. " For whosoever shall call on the name of the Lord shall be saved. How then shall they call on him in whom they have not believed? and how shall they believe in him of whom they have not heard? and how shall they hear without a preacher? and how shall they preach except they be sent?" (Rom. 10 : 13-15.)

Indifference to the cause of missions is

cruelty to immortal souls. How are sinners in our own land, or in foreign lands, to be saved without the gospel? Ought not those who have the gospel to send it to those who have it not? Earth's wretched millions are starving for "the bread of life," and this bread is in the custody of the churches. Dare they refuse to distribute it among the perishing at home and abroad? No church can perform its duties to the world without sustaining the cause of missions—without giving, according to its ability, to spread the gospel of the grace of God. Praying without giving is presumption, and giving without praying indicates a self-dependence offensive to God. Let it be said, as of Cornelius, so of every church: "Thy prayers and thine alms are come up as a memorial before God." When prayers and alms go together, there is a happy conjunction.

NOTE.—The subject of this chapter—Duties of a Church—might be expanded into volumes. Our narrow limits have required its compression. It may be said, in conclusion, that a church with the New Testament for its charter of incorporation, is *constitutionally* a society, organized for the promotion of Christian objects. These objects should be prosecuted so zealously by all church-members as to make it apparent that no secret or secular organization is needed to carry forward any benevolent or Christian work. And besides, whatever good church-members do, should be done in their *Christian* character.

APPENDIX

I. BUSINESS MEETINGS OF A CHURCH, ASSOCIATIONS, ETC.

WHERE the spirit of Christian love and courtesy prevails, very few rules are necessary in the transaction of church business. The pastor of a church, by virtue of his office, is its moderator. He therefore presides at its meetings, which should be opened with singing, reading a suitable portion of Scripture, and prayer. The clerk then reads the minutes of the last meeting, and the pastor states, that if there is no motion to amend, the minutes will stand approved. If corrections are necessary, they are made, that the records may show exactly what has been done. The items of business should be taken up thus: 1. Unfinished business; 2. Reports from committees; 3. New business. It is not necessary to make a motion to take up unfinished business. It is before the church and must be acted on, unless a motion to postpone its consideration prevails. So of reports from committees. Under the item of new business any brother can mention what, in his judgment, claims the consideration of the church; but in all matters of importance it is desirable that there should be some previous consultation among the most prudent brethren as to what new business shall be introduced. Nothing has been said as to the time of receiving members, because some churches prefer that this shall be done directly after the devotional exercises; others that it shall be done after all other business is transacted; while others, still, receive members, not at business, but at covenant and prayer meetings.

CONCERNING MOTIONS

A motion made, and not seconded, does not claim the moderator's notice; but if seconded, he must state it to the meeting. This must be done before there is any discussion.

While a motion is undergoing discussion no new motion can be presented. But it is in order to move to amend a motion by adding or striking out words, phrases, and sentences. It is even parliamentary to move to amend by striking out all after the word *Resolved,* and introducing new matter in conflict with the original proposition. This, however, is not an amendment, but a substitute. An amendment must be germane to the matter embraced in the motion: a substitute is intended to supersede it.

Some suppose a motion can be withdrawn by the mover any time before the vote is taken. Others think that after a motion comes regularly before the meeting it cannot be withdrawn except by consent of the body. The practice of deliberative bodies is conforming more and more to the latter view. Unanimous consent, however, is not necessary.

When an amendment to a motion is accepted by the mover no vote on the amendment is to be taken; if the mover does not accept it, a separate vote must be taken on the amendment, and then on the original proposition.

It is in order to move an amendment to an amendment, but this is the utmost limit to which the matter can go, and seldom should go so far.

PRIVILEGED QUESTIONS

These embrace motions to adjourn, to lay on the table, to have the previous question, to amend, to commit, to postpone. They are called privileged because, it is supposed, they can be made at any time. This, however, is not strictly true; for even the question of adjournment, which takes precedence of all other questions, cannot be presented while a member is speaking, or a vote is being taken; nor can a motion to adjourn, which has been negatived, be renewed until some other proposition is made, or other business is transacted.[1]

It will rarely be necessary in the transaction of business in churches, associations, etc., to call for the previous question. When, however, a motion for the previous question is made and seconded, the moderator will say, " Shall the main question now be put? " If the decision is affirmative, the meeting votes, without further discussion, on the original

---

[1] Writers on Parliamentary Rules differ as to what are privileged questions. Jefferson, in his " Manual," includes all named above except the " previous question." Matthias, in his " Rules of Order," embraces all except the motion to lay on the table. Cushing, in his " Manual," reduces privileged questions to three, namely: adjournment, questions of privilege, and orders of the day; while he ranks as " Subsidiary Questions " the following: Lie on the table, previous question, postponement, commitment, amendment.

motion. If the meeting decides that the main question shall not be put—it indicates a desire that the discussion shall go on.

NOT DEBATABLE

Certain motions are not debatable, such as the motion to *adjourn*, to have the *previous question*, to *lay on the table*, etc.

But when these motions are modified by some condition of *time, place,* or *purpose,* they become debatable.

MOTIONS TO RECONSIDER

A motion to reconsider a proposition formerly adopted must be made by one who voted with the majority. If such a motion prevails, the original matter is before the body, as if it had never been acted on.

POINTS OF ORDER, APPEAL

If a member in debate violates any recognized rule of order, it is the business of the moderator to call him to order. Or, any other member may present a point of order, which the moderator must decide. If the decision is unsatisfactory, an appeal may be taken to the body; but this should be done only in peculiar cases.

MISCELLANEOUS MATTERS

In stating a motion or taking a vote the moderator should rise from his seat.

If there is an equal division of votes, the moderator may give the casting vote, or he may, more prudently in most cases, decline voting. If he declines, the matter is decided in the negative. It is not desirable for any question that comes before a church to be decided by a majority of *one* vote, and for that vote to be the pastor's.

No member can speak except on some definite subject before the body unless he wishes to explain why he is about to make a motion. It is generally better to make a motion and then, after it is seconded, speak in explanation and defence of it.

When blanks are to be filled, if different numbers are proposed, the vote must be taken first on the largest number, the longest time, etc.

If a deliberative body decides beforehand to adjourn at a certain hour, when that hour comes the moderator, without waiting for a motion to adjourn, must pronounce the meeting adjourned.

II. FORMS OF MINUTES, LETTERS, ETC.

There are no invariable forms, but the following are recommended as generally suitable:

1. RECORD OF CHURCH MEETING

[Place, Date]

The ——— church met for business at — o'clock, the pastor presiding. After devotional exercises the minutes of the last meeting were read and approved. [After this whatever business is done must be recorded.]

Adjourned.

——— ———, Clerk.

2. Letter of Dismission

[Place, Date]

The —— Baptist church of ——.

    To her sister, the —— Baptist church of ——

Dear Brethren:

    This certifies that —— —— is a member with us in good standing and full fellowship. At —— own request —— is hereby dismissed from us to unite with you. When received by you —— connection with us will terminate.

    By order of the church.

—— ——, Church Clerk.

This letter will be valid for —— months.

3. Letter of Notification

[Place, Date]

    To the —— church.

Dear Brethren:

    You are hereby notified that —— —— **was** received by letter from you to membership in the —— church, —— ——

—— ——, Church Clerk.

4. Letters of Commendation

    These are usually given by pastors to members **who** expect to be absent from home for a time. **They are** substantially as follows:

[Place, Date]

    This certifies that —— —— is a member **of** the —— Baptist church **in** this place, in **good** standing, and is commended to the Christian fellowship of all sister churches. ——— ———,

Pastor ——— Baptist church.

5. CALL FOR A COUNCIL OF RECOGNITION

[Place, Date]

To the ——— Baptist church in ———.
Dear Brethren:

There is a company of brethren and sisters in the Lord who wish to become an independent church. You are therefore requested to send your pastor and two brethren to meet in council at ——— ——— at — o'clock, to take the matter into consideration. If the council approves the movement, said brethren and sisters will be glad to have the moral influence of its recognition. The following churches are invited to send messengers. ———, ———, ———, ———, ———.

Yours, truly,

——— ———,
——— ———,
——— ———,
Committee.

6. CALL FOR A COUNCIL OF ORDINATION

[Place, Date]

The ——— Baptist church of ———.
To the ——— Baptist church of ———.
Dear Brethren:

We request you to send your pastor and two brethren to meet in council ——— ——— at —

o'clock, to consider the propriety of ordaining to the work of the ministry brother ——— ———. The following churches are invited to send messengers : ———, ———, ———.

By order of the church,

——— ———, Clerk.

7. CALL FOR AN ADVISORY COUNCIL

[Place, Date]

The ——— Baptist church of ———.

    To the ——— Baptist church of ———.

Dear Brethren :

We are sorry to inform you that there are serious difficulties among us, disturbing our peace and hindering our usefulness as a church. We therefore request you to send your pastor and two brethren to meet in council, to advise us what to do. The following churches are invited to send messengers : ———, ———, ———, ———.

By order of the church,

——— ———, Clerk.

8. RECORD OF A COUNCIL

[Place, Date]

A council, called by the ——— church, met ——————, at — o'clock. Brother ——— ——— was chosen moderator, and brother ——— ·———, clerk. Prayer by ——— ———. The church records, referring to the call of the council, were read, from which it appears that the object is ——— ——— ——— ——— ——————. The credentials of the messengers were presented. The following churches sent the following brethren, namely:

CHURCHES.   MESSENGERS.

[Whatever is done must be faithfully recorded.] On motion the council was dissolved.

———— ————, Moderator.
———— ————, Clerk.

9. FORM OF MINISTERIAL LICENSE

[Place, Date]

This is to certify, that brother ———— ———— is a member of the ———— Baptist church, in good standing and full fellowship. Trusting that God has called him to preach the gospel, we hereby license him to engage in the great work; and we offer to God our earnest prayers that he may become "a workman that needeth not to be ashamed, rightly dividing the word of truth."

By order of the church, this ———— day of ————

———— ————, Pastor.
———— ————, Clerk.

10. CERTIFICATE OF ORDINATION

This is to certify that brother ———— ———— was ordained to the work of the gospel ministry, by prayer and the laying on of the hands of the eldership, on the ———— day of ————, 18—. He was called to ordination by the ———— church of which he was a member, which had ample opportunity to become acquainted with his piety and ministerial gifts.

The ordaining council was composed of —— brethren from —— churches, who after a deliberate and thorough examination of the candidate cordially recommended him for ordination.

Our beloved brother, the bearer of this paper, has, therefore, the entire approbation of the ordaining council in being publicly set apart to preach the gospel and administer the ordinances of Christ.

May he, like Barnabas, be "full of the Holy Spirit and of faith," and through him may "much people be added to the Lord."

—— ——, Moderator,
—— ——, Clerk.

III. MARRIAGE CEREMONY

Marriage is an institution of divine appointment, given in wisdom and kindness, to increase human happiness and to support social order.

In the Bible, which should be the lamp to your path in every relation, you will find the directions needed in this.

In token of your decided choice of each other as partners for life, you —— —— and —— —— will please to unite your right hands.

(Joining of hands.)

Do you solemnly promise, before Almighty God and these witnesses, to receive each other as husband and wife, agreeing to perform the duties growing out of the relation, pledging yourselves to love each other, and to make every reasonable exertion to promote each other's happiness until the union into which you are now entering is dissolved by death?

(*When a ring is employed the following can be used.* In confirmation of these vows, you will please give and receive this ring, as an emblem and pledge of the pure and enduring love you have promised to cherish for each other.)

In view of the promises thus made, I do now, by virtue of the authority vested in me, as a minister of the gospel, pronounce you husband and wife, henceforth in interest and destiny, as in affection, ONE. And what God hath joined together, let **not** man put asunder.

IV. THE PROVINCE OF ASSOCIATIONS AND COUNCILS

It is customary among Baptists for the churches, according to their convenience, to form District ASSOCIATIONS. These bodies are composed of messengers from the churches. And as no fixed number of churches is necessary in organizing an association, it may be either large or small. Every church acts voluntarily in connecting itself with an association. There is not—there cannot be—compulsion in the matter. This results from the fact that the Scriptures recognize no higher tribunal than a church.

There are many prudential reasons for the formation of associations. Some persons seem to think that the chief business of associations is to collect the statistics of the churches and publish them. This is the least part of their business. Their great work is connected with local Church Extension, the Missionary Enterprise, Bible, Book, and Tract Distribution, Ministerial Education, and the Sunday School work. Combined action for these objects is more effective than isolated action. This is the supreme reason for associations.

It follows, of necessity, that an association is only an advisory body. It may recommend to the churches that they do thus and thus; but it can go no further. It can enact no decrees; and if it did, it would have no power to execute them. It is no Court of Appeals, whose decisions are to nullify those of the churches. Bpatists must, with holy jealousy, watch and arrest the first encroachments of associations on the independence of the churches.

There needs to be something said about COUNCILS. Like associations, they are advisory bodies; and while this fact is kept distinctly in view, their utility cannot be questioned; but there is danger lest they assume authority over the churches; and lest the churches acquiesce in the assumption. The following remarks on councils, from a judicious author,[1] are recommended to the Christian brotherhood:

"The true theory of councils appears to be that which regards them as merely advisory. In ordinary cases of discipline, involving no doubtful or difficult question, they are not needed. But cases of a dif-

[1] Rev. Warnam Walker, in his "Church Discipline," pp. 63. 64.

ferent character may arise. A church may be called to act upon questions of the highest importance, and so complicated and difficult, as to render needful all the wisdom and experience that can be brought to bear upon them. Or, a church may be so divided in opinion on questions seriously affecting its vital interests, that no approach to unanimity can reasonably be hoped for, except through the influence of such a council as may command the respect and confidence of the body. Or, the pastor of a church may be guilty of some misconduct, involving a forfeiture of his ministerial and Christian character. In this last case, although no doubt may be entertained in relation to the course to be pursued, still it is important that the advice of other pastors and able brethren should be obtained. The removal of one of Zion's watchmen is a matter of painful interest, not merely to the one church over which he presides, but to many. As a public teacher of religion, he has had a place in their affectionate regard; and his fall, like the extinction of a star, is felt by them to be a public calamity. It would seem, therefore, in the case supposed, to be due to the neighboring churches, that before any decisive action is had, a council should be called to deliberate upon the whole matter, and say what action in their judgment is advisable. The opinion of such a body, although not binding upon the church, is entitled to its consideration; and if adopted must add greatly to the weight of its final decision.

"In this, and in all cases, where the aid of a council is sought, the right of a decision rests with the church. It is the province of the council, not to act authoritatively, but to advise the churches how to act. The advice so given ought by no means to be lightly rejected; but if, in the deliberative judgment of the church, it is contrary to the will of the Master, it cannot be adopted. When a disagreement of this kind exists, perhaps the most effective means of restoring harmony may be to have recourse to a second council. Still, the ultimate decision belongs to the church.

"It is supposed by some that the power of ordination to the Christian ministry resides, not in the church, but in a council, assembled at the call of a church, and acting through a presbytery of its own selection. And this being assumed, it is supposed to follow, that the power to depose from the ministry, which is an act of equal authority with the other, must be lodged in a body similarly constituted. But whence, it may be demanded, does the council, as such, derive its origin and its power? Evidently from the church. But for the call of the church it would never have existed. It is the creature of the church, and cannot, without manifest impropriety, exercise an authority superior to that of its creator. Besides—if a church be incompetent to depose from the ministry, it must also be incompetent to exclude a minister, since the former act is virtually included in the latter. The discipline of the church, so far as ministers are concerned, would thus become an empty name. The truth seems to be that the ordinary power is in the church. Inasmuch, however, as the exrcise of that power is an act of public importance and interest, it is due to the neighboring churches, that the advice of their pastors and such other members as they may designate for this purpose, should previously be heard. Especially is it due to the presbyters who may be called upon to act, that they should have opportunity to satisfy themselves in relation to the character, call to the ministry, and qualifications of the candidate. For these reasons, a council ought always in such cases to be called, not to ordain, but to advise the church in respect to ordination; nor is it easy to conceive of a case in which it would be expedient for the church to insist upon proceeding, contrary to such advice. Still, the right of decision is in the church; and the officiating presbytery should be regarded as acting, not in behalf of the council, but in behalf of the church."

This long extract has been made, because the views it presents are believed to be of great importance. Councils composed of judicious brethren may be expected to give good advice, and good advice should be taken; but as councils are advisory, they are not authoritative bodies. Hence for a council to require a church to give a pledge beforehand to abide by its decision is a direct assault on church independence. And for a church to give such a pledge is disloyalty to Christ; for it is a surrender of the great principle that a church is the highest tribunal, and is the only competent authority to pronounce a final decision.

V. BAPTIST DECLARATIONS OF FAITH

The Declaration of Faith contained on pages 43-61 was widely used by Baptists of the United States during the second half of the nineteenth century. It is often referred to as "The New Hampshire Confession." While the influence of this statement has continued into the twentieth century, major changes have been made by some Baptist groups. The Southern Baptist Convention, for example, adopted a modified form in 1925. In 1963 it adopted a much-more revised form under the title "The Baptist Faith and Message." Both the 1925 and the 1963 statements may be found in the *Annual of the Southern Baptist Convention* for 1963. The Baptist Sunday School Board, Nashville, Tennessee, also has published the 1963 statement in tract form. A Baptist church being constituted in the twentieth century should consider these or other appropriate revisions before adopting a declaration of its own.

INDEX

NOTES

NOTES

NOTES

NOTES

NOTES

NOTES

NOTES

NOTES